ISBN: 978-0-578-64968-9
Printed in PRC

THE
WILSON CREEK
STORY

MICK WILSON

CONTENTS

INTRODUCTION

"Someone has to write this story down; it's too good not to be shared."

My friend Steve and I were sitting in our winery's courtyard. I had just given him a twenty-minute version of how the winery started.

His reaction was similar to that of others who've heard our story:

"I can identify with your family. The Wilson family isn't perfect either."

"This isn't how wineries usually start!"

"Your story gives me hope that maybe I can also take some big risks in life."

Risks. That's a big part of the Wilson Creek story. It wasn't always certain that the risks would pay off, but we persevered. And slowly, we began to see the rewards.

So I decided to take on the task of documenting our journey. I interviewed family members and key players in the story. I compiled older family interviews and dug up old photos and articles.

We didn't have the kind of budget that would normally be required for such a venture, and we didn't have the winemaking pedigree that would give us automatic prestige in the industry. We did, however, have a few secret weapons: a commitment to family, hard work, persistence, and a natural desire to connect with all kinds of people. We also brought a quality that has always been present in our family: an attitude of generous, open hospitality. That open-hearted attitude is what made our family home a gathering place for neighbors and friends. It's what our guests feel now as they stroll through the Wilson Creek Winery, sipping award-winning wines and enjoying the ambiance.

In the following pages, you'll meet the members of my family who embarked on this extraordinary adventure together—and succeeded against all the odds.

There are Gerry and Rosie, my parents, who have always provided the support and inspiration we needed. There's my older brother, Bill, the hard-driving entrepreneur who initiated the whole idea and made sure we didn't quit. Without Bill and his wife, Jenifer, there would be no Wilson Creek. My younger sister, Libby, and her husband, Craig, were involved and integral at each step, including helping with large events and sales. My wife, Deanna joined the business a few years after we opened and launched our distribution. And there are all the friends, siblings, in-laws, nieces, and nephews who also made invaluable contributions. And there's me, a family member and co-owner who was part of it all from the beginning. Now I have the privilege of telling the story—a story of how our family, amid triumphs and struggles, endured through it all—together.

Sip back and enjoy!

Mick Wilson

- Mick Wilson

A MOMENT TO REFLECT

"Excuse me, may I interrupt?"

The man's voice startled me. My wife, Deanna, and I were enjoying lunch in our restaurant at the winery, the Creekside Grille, with my parents, Gerry and Rosie. I turned and saw a man with a glass of sparkling wine in his hand and a grin on his face.

"I just want to tell you all—thanks for creating this winery!"

Gerry and Rosie stopped and listened intently as the man continued. "We're from San Diego," he said. "I'm a Wine Club Member. I have been coming here for years. I just love the ambiance, your wines, the family, the staff—and of course, the dogs. Wilson Creek is my happy place."

Gerry smiled. "Well, thank you for supporting us!"

Wait a minute—he's thanking us for having this business?

He shook our hands and took a selfie with Rosie and Gerry. After lunch, Deanna and I walked around the busy courtyard for a bit. The midday summer sun warmed my shoulders. Geranium balls atop the wine barrels added their scent to the hundreds of snapdragons nearby. I noticed about 150 people interacting in the courtyard while the arching white bridge accented the spray from the pond's fountain. Waves of laughter rose above the sound of a three-piece band playing soft rock in the background. At one of the tables, four couples popped a bottle of Almond Champagne and clinked their glasses. A bride posed for photos in the nearby vineyard, preparing for her ceremony later that evening.

"Wow," I commented to Deanna, "this is pretty special!" She smiled and nodded.

I saw Rosie and Gerry talking with guests in the Creekside Grille. Two young couples played bocce ball in front of the ballroom patio. Over at the winery entrance,

2019

my older brother, Bill, greeted guests as they entered. Bill's wife, Jenifer, worked with a cashier in the tasting room, putting price tags on gift shop items. The second-floor Wine Club patio overflowed with members enjoying their free wine tastings. My sister, Libby, and her husband, Craig, led a tour of twelve people through the nearby vineyard. The whole scene felt magical! I loved the energetic, casual, fun vibe.

I need to do this more—stop and reflect. Why are so many people enjoying this winery? How did we get here?

When we opened our tasting room in 2000, three Wilson families lived in three mobile homes in our vineyards. Our tasting room had one 20-foot bar and two small restrooms with one toilet each. Our first crew consisted of seven Wilsons, five part-time staff, and more than 40 volunteers who helped whenever they could. The parking lot had 30 regular spaces and two handicapped spots. Our five-year goal was to serve 250 guests in a week and produce 5,000 cases of wine. The goal seemed audacious. We couldn't imagine a winery that large.

Now, 20 years later, we are astonished at where we have come. Our staff of 250 serves our guests, who average more than 1500 on a typical Saturday—1200 in the tasting room alone. Parking has been expanded to 300 spaces. We serve guests on twelve tasting bars that total over 400 linear feet.

We now produce over 100,000 cases annually, and our wines are consistently rated 90+ out of 100. We farm more than 200 acres of vines, and our sparkling wines are on store shelves in 35 states. We have been consistently voted by the readers of the *Press Enterprise* as the most popular winery in the Inland Empire. Along the way, we've been able to give back to our community in numerous ways.

Somehow, we did all this without our family coming apart. We've had our struggles, but we still love each other and enjoy our time together. Four generations of Wilsons live within 15 minutes of the winery. Gerry and Rosie feel they are experiencing "heaven on earth."

What follows is the story of what it took to get us to where we are today, as a family and as a business—the frustrations, hardships, joys, and victories.

But the story really began in 1952, when some seemingly random events brought two extraordinary people together.

LEFT PAGE TOP: 2018 Family Photo. LEFT TO RIGHT: Bill, Jenifer, Cambria, Cassidy, Deanna, Mick, Sarah, Gerry, Libby, Rosie, Craig, Gavin, Hayden, Heather, Luke, Chris, Chloe, Crew, Jessica, Jett. DOGS: Tipsy, Sauvy, Sadie, Chablis. BOTTOM LEFT: 2019 Courtyard Bar & Grill. BOTTOM RIGHT: Tasting Room 2019.

WHEN GERRY MET ROSIE

Rosie Iverson's roommate needed a date for a party. Rosie asked her good friend, Bob, for some help.

"Say, why don't I fix your roommate up with an officer friend of mine?" Bob said. "This guy is caring, generous, and gracious. We live in the same barracks." Bob was an Air Force officer stationed at Mountain Home Air Force Base in the desert near Boise. Rosie had recently moved to the area from Iowa. She was young, a civilian—and single.

"He's a guy I trust," Bob continued. "His name is Gerry Wilson." He paused for a moment. "Come to think of it, *you* should meet Gerry."

"Really?" Rosie didn't reveal her interest right away. She had come to Boise to establish an Easter Seals Center. After graduating from Iowa State, numerous recruiters wanted to hire Rosie. She chose the position in Boise because it fit well with her other passion—snow skiing.

"Yeah," Bob continued, "I think you two would make a good couple. He's tall, blonde, and likes classical music—pretty much the same things you like."

A few days later, Rosie noticed a photo in a Boise newspaper of two Air Force officers and two nurses, all in uniform. She could not see the faces clearly, but the caption had various names in it. What stuck out to Rosie were the words, "Gerry Wilson, from Minneapolis, decorating the officers' club for the annual Christmas party."

TOP: Gerry at a party in the Beta Theta Pi Fraternity House at the University of Minnesota. BOTTOM: Rosie and Gerry caught in the vines. RIGHT PAGE: TOP: Union Pacific Railroad postcard from the 1950s. CENTER: A typical Pullman Train Dining Car 1950s.

EASTBOUND TRAIN

One week later, Rosie boarded an early morning train from Boise to Ames, Iowa. It was Christmastime, and she couldn't wait to see her family. A boyfriend awaited her back home, but in their months apart, their relationship fizzled. She boarded the Pullman sleeper car at 5:00 a.m., found her bunk, and slowly drifted off. A few hours later she entered the sitting car and noticed two handsome Air Force lieutenants sitting across the aisle. It was not her habit to talk to strangers, but this time she did. The glistening opal ring on her left ring finger could have given the impression that she was married. The officers greeted Rosie and they started chatting with her.

The train originated in Portland, Oregon, so Rosie assumed the handsome lieutenant was stationed there. But he surprised her. "I'm stationed in Mountain Home, not far from Boise," he said.

"Oh, you poor guy," Rosie chuckled; she knew the base sat in the middle of the bleak Idaho desert.

He looked intrigued. "How do you know about Mountain Home?"

"I grew up in Iowa. But now I work in Boise."

As the train meandered through the rolling countryside near Pocatello, the lieutenant peered out the window.

"Look at all those pine trees," he mused. "A few days ago, I went to the nearby mountains to cut down a tree for our officers' club Christmas party."

Suddenly, the newspaper photo she'd seen flashed through Rosie's mind. "Where did you say you were originally from?"

"I didn't, but I'm from Minneapolis."

Her brain raced as she connected the dots. She looked at the lieutenant, flashed a sly smile, and asked, "Are you by any chance Gerry Wilson?"

His jaw dropped as his mind whirled. *How did she know my name? Who is this pretty woman? Have we met before?*

Rosie saw the shock on his face. *Oh no*, she thought, *I must've scared him to death!* She laughed and told him about the newspaper photo. The three of them chatted over lunch in the dining car and spent the rest of the afternoon together until Gerry changed trains in Omaha. He was on Christmas leave to visit his family in Minneapolis. Rosie traveled on to Iowa and spent the holidays with her family. She and her old boyfriend never connected, but it didn't matter. She knew she had just met the man she wanted to marry.

12

DEEP ROOTS

MISS ROSEMARY IVERSON of 924 Franklin street has been appointed teacher at the Easter Seal center of the Idaho Crippled Children's society. The center will be opened in September at Fifth and Grove streets.

Rosie & Gerry

Rosie Iverson grew up as the youngest of four kids in Ames, the home of Iowa State University, where her dad was a well-known professor. Being a tomboy, she often played football with the neighborhood boys in her family's big backyard—usually as the quarterback. She was also an accomplished figure skater and played a mean game of hockey. Rosie learned to play piano at six and even performed on the radio as a teenager. But soon, cheerleading, boys, and school activities became higher priorities.

As a teenager, Rosie detasseled corn each summer—a hard but fun job. Beginning in high school, Rosie knew she wanted to work with disabled children. After investigating her college choices, she chose Iowa State for its outstanding child development program. Rosie thrived at ISU, participating in numerous campus organizations, and the prestigious Mortar Board Honor Society. During college, she volunteered at a hospital in Des Moines in their children's ward. She took a semester internship at the Cerebral Palsy Center in Detroit, Michigan. While there, Rosie began her lifelong hobby of snow skiing.

Upon graduating, Rosie received calls from several recruiters. One of them asked a staffer at the Iowa State personnel department how she might attract Rosie to her organization. "Number one," the official responded, "you have to have a ski hill nearby. If there isn't one, then build one!" Rosie's love of skiing led her to accept a position at the new Easter Seals Center in Boise, Idaho, which happened to be near the Sun Valley Ski Resort. She immersed herself in her work, designing the center, painting circus murals on the walls, raising funds, and lecturing throughout the state about cerebral palsy. Her Midwestern values of frugality, hard work, and neighborly compassion contributed to her success.

Gerry's path had been markedly different. Born in Montana in 1930, he experienced the full impact of the Great Depression. When his family couldn't afford new shoes, he cut cardboard to slide between his socks and the holes in his soles. Sadly, when he was three, his pregnant mother fell down their basement stairs and passed away. His father, who managed the local hardware store, remarried two years later. Gerry eventually became the eldest of four children. The family moved to Devils Lake, North Dakota, and then to Minneapolis, Minnesota.

TOP LEFT: Rosemary Iverson's high school graduation photo. TOP RIGHT: A 1952 article announcing Rosemary Iverson as teacher at the Easter Seals Center of Idaho Crippled Children's Society. RIGHT PAGE: TOP LEFT: High school graduation photo of Gerry. TOP RIGHT: Gerry on college graduation day.

When Gerry was eleven, World War II began.

"When the war came along, the hardware business went *kerplunk*," Gerry recalls. "You couldn't sell any appliances—there were none to sell." His father took a job building gun controllers for battleships and later became a stockbroker. His dad's solid work ethic became a great example to Gerry, who learned the value of having a job and appreciated his father's influential role in his life.

At 13 years old, Gerry started working and buying his own clothes. During his teenage years, he always had a job. Each job felt like a new adventure for him. He scrubbed floors, painted houses, delivered newspapers, stocked supermarket shelves, shoveled sidewalks, cleaned Dairy Queen machines at night, caddied for golfers, operated a hospital elevator, swept a beauty shop floor, sold magazines door-to-door, and worked in a cafeteria where he could eat all he wanted.

The war ended when Gerry was 15, and jobs were plentiful for men. The railroad companies began employing boys as young as 16 years old. A friend told him, "The railroad is hiring, and they pay forty-five cents an hour! Plus, when it rains, we can eat watermelon in the rail cars!" Gerry wasn't old enough, but the opportunity was too good to pass up, so both boys lied about their ages and went to work at the local rail yard. They soon found themselves spiking, tamping, and moving railroad ties caked with creosote, the tar-like substance used to make the wood stronger. They lifted metal rails that weighed 80 pounds per foot. All the rail workers drank out of a central water keg. Many of the men chewed tobacco, which tended to drip into the water when they drank. The barrel was disgusting, but after working long hours under the

hot sun, Gerry viewed that nasty water as the nectar of the gods. After a long day, the younger workers would often cool down by jumping off of a bridge into the lake. But the promise of watermelon proved to be a mirage; sadly, it never rained a single day that summer.

The drudgery never dampened Gerry's ambition. "I looked up at this engineer when the diesel engine came by, and he looked down on us," he recalls. "We were sweating, we were covered in creosote, and I said, 'Someday I want his job!'" When Gerry turned 16, he hitchhiked to California with his best friend. They found work as irrigators and tractor drivers on a 5,000-acre asparagus ranch in the San Joaquin Valley, a job that kept them busy for two summers.

As a teen in Minnesota, Gerry was popular but unaware of it. The neighborhood girls knew he often walked from his home to the movie theater with his buddies, so they would wait near his front steps, hoping he'd stroll by and invite them along. "Hi girls," he'd say—and keep walking. Looking back later, Gerry said to himself, *How oblivious can you be?*

When it came time to enter college, Gerry enrolled at the University of Minnesota, where he was elected Snow King and selected to the honor society. He sang baritone in the prestigious University of Minnesota Chorus and served as president of the Beta Theta Pi Fraternity. He became a leader in the University Air Force ROTC program and graduated as an officer. Like Rosie, Gerry Wilson exemplified the virtues of the Midwest: he was hardworking, humble, honest, faithful, frugal, and friendly.

WESTBOUND TRAIN

After a relaxing Christmas with her family, Rosie boarded the train back to Boise. She remembered that Gerry would be taking a train back to Boise about the same time, so she asked the porter if anyone was boarding in Omaha. He looked at his manifest and pointed out several berths next to hers reserved for Omaha passengers. "By chance," Rosie asked, "Is there anyone by the name of *Gerry Wilson* on the list?"

The porter scanned his manifest again. "Yes," he said, pointing at the sleeper bunk right next to hers. "That one's his."

Rosie grinned.

As she lay in her upper bed, Rosie's thoughts turned to Omaha, where the Minneapolis train would be stopping. She hoped Gerry would get on! She was still modest, so while she waited, she put a coat over her robe and took the rollers out of her hair.

Near midnight, the train stopped in Omaha to pick up the Minneapolis passengers. The lone ceiling light in the sleeper car cast a faint glow. In her bunk with the curtains closed, Rosie listened intently as the passengers boarded. When the first person entered the sleeper car, she recognized Gerry's voice. Her heart raced. When she discerned

he was a few feet away, Rosie popped her head out from the curtains. "Lieutenant Wilson!"

"Who's that?"

Rosie responded calmly, "What woman would be saying 'Lieutenant Wilson' to you from an upper bunk on a train?"

Wearing a full uniform and a big grin, Gerry set down his canvas bag and walked the few steps to her bunk. He pulled down the little wooden ladder, climbed up a few rungs, put his elbows on the edge of Rosie's mattress, and gently said, "Hi, Rosie!"

They chatted for a half-hour, and then Gerry went to his bunk, smiling.

The next morning a porter found Gerry shaving in the bathroom. "Excuse me, sir, are you Lieutenant Wilson?"

"Yes, I am," he said, dabbing his neck. "How can I help you?"

"Well, good morning, sir. I want to pass on an important message to you. A lovely woman is waiting for you in the dining car, and she would love for you to join her. Our Union Pacific French Toast is world-famous, ya know!"

Gerry felt elated. He got dressed and walked to the dining car with a slight pep in his step. He took in the aromas of fresh coffee, warm maple syrup, and bacon. He scanned the tables, then locked eyes with Rosie. She sat at a booth for two next to a large window that captured the passing Midwest scenery. The bright morning sun accented her hair and delicate smile. They enjoyed a French toast breakfast together and then spent the day getting better acquainted.

When the train arrived at Boise, Rosie invited Gerry and his friend to her apartment for coffee that evening. Gerry had to get to the base, so Rosie gave him her number before he left. Even after the enchanting train ride, Gerry didn't call for a week. Rosie was discouraged—she thought she had met *the one*. The next Saturday, Gerry called and apologized for not contacting her as he had been sick all week with food poisoning from the train. He then told her about a party at the officers' club that night. "Can you go? I know it is last minute."

"Sure," she said, grinning from ear to ear.

"I'm glad you can make it!" Gerry exclaimed. "I don't have a car, but I'll find a ride into Boise and pick you up." The base was 65 miles away. By the end of the day, Gerry couldn't find a ride, because all of the other officers had already left for Boise. He called Rosie and told her the bad news.

Rosie hung up and told her roommate what had happened. "Well," said her roommate, "Why don't you just drive to the base in your car?"

"I can't do *that*!" Rosie exclaimed. "It would be too forward."

But she wanted to see Gerry. Fortunately, Gerry called a half-hour later. Rosie mustered her courage and asked, "Would it be too forward of me to drive out to the base?"

"No, it would be great! I'll alert the guards at the entrance. I'll be waiting at the officers' club, and they'll call me when you arrive."

That night Rosie drove alone on the dark, empty highway. As she approached the dimly-lit gate, her heart raced in anticipation. She announced her name to the military policeman on duty and waited while he scanned his list. To Rosie's dismay, her name was not there. Gerry told the afternoon guards of her coming, but there had been a change of shifts since then. Discouraged, she sat parked at the gate, not knowing what to do. Should she drive back to Boise? After weighing her options for a few seconds, Rosie told the guard, "I realize I am not on your list, but I'm here to meet Lieutenant Gerry Wilson for the officers' club party. Is there *any* way I can come in?"

He stared at Rosie for a long five seconds. She looked elegant in her pale blue dress and simple pearl necklace. Concluding that she was no threat, he nodded. "Okay, ma'am, the officers' club is around those barracks to the right. Have fun!" Rosie found a parking spot near the club and sat in her car in the dark, looking for any sign of Gerry. She noticed a distinguished-looking officer walking past the front of her car. She rolled down her window. "Excuse me, sir. Could I walk into the officers' club with you? I'm meeting Gerry Wilson."

"Ah, yes, Gerry Wilson," he said. "I'm his commanding officer. It would be my privilege to escort you in." The colonel offered his arm and they walked in together. Within ten seconds, Rosie saw Gerry walking toward her in his uniform. She was struck by how handsome he looked. *Yes,* she thought, *this is the man I am going to marry. He just doesn't know it yet.*

Later that evening, Gerry escorted Rosie back to Boise. He intended to book a hotel room in town and arrange a ride back to the base the next day, but he couldn't find a vacancy anywhere. In those days, unmarried couples sleeping under the same roof would raise a few eyebrows. Even though she felt a bit awkward about it, Rosie invited Gerry to sleep on the sofa in her living room, and she shared the bedroom with her roommate. To this day, she jokes, "On our first date, he spent the night!"

LEFT PAGE: TOP: Gerry (top middle) singing. He was part of the University choir. He is with members of the Grey Friars Honorary Society.
BOTTOM: As the 1952 University of Minnesota Snow King, Gerry crowns the Snow Queen. Both won elections in which a dime counted as one vote. RIGHT PAGE: Gerry in front of his Air Force squadron's logo.

TYING THE KNOT

Over the next few winter months, Rosie's apartment in Boise became the hangout for Gerry's group of officers. Her friends in Boise were mainly young, professional women, and the base was an hour away, so Rosie and her apartment became the connector of those two worlds. Gerry and his friends often stayed in the penthouse of a downtown hotel as they interacted with Rosie and her working female friends. These gatherings continued for a few months until Gerry left for a six-week temporary duty at an officer's personnel school in St. Louis.

During this time in St. Louis, Gerry and Rosie wrote and phoned each other regularly. They knew the next step would be to meet each other's families. In Boise, Rosie had already made plans to fly to Minneapolis to meet Gerry's parents over Memorial Day. And in St. Louis, Gerry brainstormed how he could meet Rosie's family in Ames, Iowa.

One particularly hot and humid day at the base, Gerry was relaxing with his friend Bill, and the conversation naturally turned to ice cream. "My girlfriend's dad makes the best ice cream!" Gerry mused.

"No," Bill said, "the best ice cream is at my alma mater—Iowa State!"

"That's funny," Gerry said. "My girlfriend's dad is a professor there. *He* is probably the top ice cream expert in the Midwest!"

Bill perked up. "Are you by any chance dating Rosie Iverson, the daughter of Professor Iverson?" Both men were astonished that they knew the same person.

Rosie Iverson's dad was an iconic leader in the dairy industry, specializing in research and development. As the head of Iowa State's dairy industry and food tech department, he gave lectures around the country and was seeking better ways of making world-class ice cream and cheese. He also started an on-campus dairy and retail center where students made and sold top-quality ice cream and cheese. Rosie likens her dad to a wine sommelier; he would examine ice cream like a wine expert analyzes a Cabernet Sauvignon.

Bill said, "Rosie and I were good friends at Iowa State and served on the Union Board together." As he and Gerry talked, Bill got an idea. "I need to go to Ames to attend a convention," he said. "Why don't you go with me? Maybe you can meet Rosie's family!"

Gerry had hoped something like this would happen; now his chance was staring him in the face. Gerry and Bill took off for Ames, Iowa. But Rosie, still in Boise, had no idea what Gerry was doing.

Professor Iverson was chatting with students at his favorite spot—the base of the towering campanile at Iowa State University. He was an imposing and dignified academician, with glasses and thick silver hair. The vibrant green grass glistened and the air was awash with the fragrant scent of May flowers. As Gerry and Bill, both in full uniform, approached Rosie's dad, Gerry felt his stomach tightening.

TOP LEFT: Iowa State University. RIGHT PAGE: LEFT: The home where Rosie grew up in Ames, Iowa.
RIGHT: Gerry's family home in Minneapolis while he was in middle school and high school.

Bill introduced himself first, then said, "Professor, I'd like you to meet Gerry Wilson."

The professor stood and looked Gerry in the eye as they shook hands. Then a broad smile came over his face. "Not *the* Gerry Wilson? Rosie told me all about you. You *must* come home and meet my wife. I'm going to call and tell her, 'Guess who's here and coming to dinner? *The* Gerry Wilson!'"

Rosie's mom prepared dinner for their new guest. Such events were normal in their home, as they often entertained faculty and foreign visitors. Rosie's sister and brother-in-law heard the news that Gerry Wilson was in town and they just "happened" to stop by the house. Her brother came over, "to get a pillow." Before the visit was over, Rosie's siblings had checked-out Gerry. But he enjoyed every minute of it.

In the middle of dinner, the phone rang. It was Rosie, calling from Boise to tell her dad about her plans to meet Gerry's parents in Minneapolis. Her dad immediately recognized Rosie's voice and handed the phone to Gerry without saying a word.

"Hi, Rosie." Gerry said.

Rosie assumed it was her brother-in-law. Slightly annoyed, she said, "John, I don't want to be rude, but I am paying for this call, so could you please put Dad on?"

Her dad took the phone back and said, "Do you know who you were just talking to?"

"Yes—John, of course!"

Her dad enunciated for effect. "No … that … was … Gerry… Wilson."

"You could have knocked me over with a feather," Rosie recalls now. As far as she knew, Gerry was still in St. Louis. "I let out a whoop in Boise that I think you could hear in Iowa! *I knew I had him.*"

Rosie started to do some homework—*just in case* Gerry proposed. She called her church in Boise to see which dates were open. Over the next few weeks, their phone conversations had turned from "*If* we get married" to "*When* we get married." And now it was time for *her* to meet *his* parents.

On Memorial Day weekend, Gerry met Rosie's plane at the Minneapolis airport. When they walked into Gerry's house, his dad greeted them, looked at Rosie, then turned to Gerry with a grin. "Ya did good, son."

Gerry recalled later, "Rosie hit it off with my dad and mom, as she does with everybody. My parents adored her."

Over the next couple of days in Minneapolis, Gerry and Rosie's conversations focused more and more on marriage. But he hadn't proposed. It was Memorial Day evening, and Rosie was set to return to Iowa the next day. Gerry walked her to the car, and as they stopped at the curb, Rosie decided to turn the discussion to possible wedding dates. During their conversation, she abruptly interjected, "How about August second, in Boise?"

"Uh … well, sure!"

As Gerry knew, people in sales call this an "assumptive close." Was this the moment? Right then and there, by the car in front of his house, Rosie insisted he get down on one knee. As they both chuckled, Gerry took her hand and asked, "Will you marry me?"

Rosie gleefully responded, "Of course."

As she puts it now, "I chased Gerry until he caught me." She knew he was the one before he did. Eight months after they met on the train, Rosie and Gerry were married.

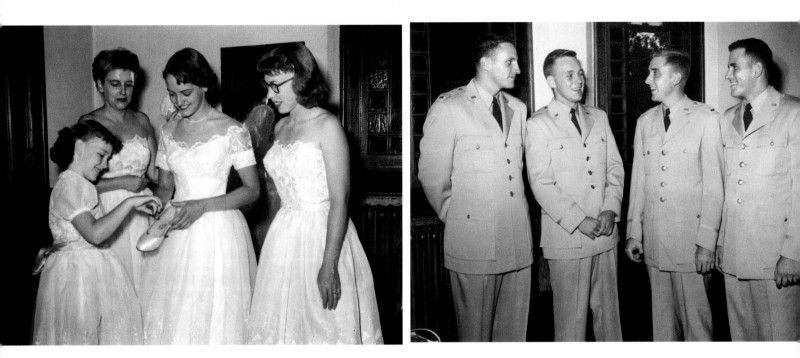

WEDDING DAY

The gray skies and cold Idaho winds on August 2, 1954 contrasted with the warmth and joy inside Boise Presbyterian Church. Gerry, his best man, and groomsmen looked sharp in their Air Force uniforms. Rosie wore an ankle-length white gown while her attendants wore aqua dresses of the same fabric. Parents and relatives from both sides attended. After the ceremony, the newlyweds honeymooned in Sun Valley, Idaho, and Yellowstone National Park. Then they went to Great Falls, Montana—Gerry's new Air Force assignment.

Two months later, things changed when Gerry received new orders: he was to report to the Fifth Air Force in three weeks. Rosie recalls, "I had no idea where the Fifth Air Force was based. To my dismay, I soon found out it was Kimpo Field, Korea. I couldn't believe we were only married for three months when the Air Force deployed Gerry to the Korean War."

When Gerry deployed, Rosie moved to Ames to be with her family. During their year apart, Rosie and Gerry wrote to each other daily, sharing their thoughts and

plans for the future. Rosie typed her letters at the kitchen table every night after dinner and mailed them the next day. She would often send brownies and Jiffy Pop popcorn, which Gerry and his tent-mates cooked over the tent's cast-iron heater. Gerry wrote and mailed a letter to Rosie every day. While in Korea, Gerry began to think he might like working in finance, like his dad. So Gerry enrolled in a correspondence course from the Securities and Exchange Commission and studied for the stockbroker exam he would take when he arrived back in the States.

Rosie had a job with Iowa State's television and media department, which ran the first college-owned station in the nation. She worked full-time as the assistant to the director of TV education. She helped produce shows and taught university students about studio work and production.

Mr. and Mrs. C. A. Iverson of Ames, Iowa, have announced the engagement and approaching marriage of their daughter, Miss Rosemary Iverson, to Lt. Gerald R. Wilson, son of Mr. and Mrs. R. W. Wilson of Minneapolis.

The wedding will be performed on Aug. 2 in the First Presbyterian church here.

Miss Iverson, a graduate of Iowa State college, is employed as child development specialist at the Easter Seal center here. In college Miss Iverson was a Pi Beta Phi sorority member, and belonged to Phi Upsilon Omicron and Mortar board. She is also a PEO member.

Lieutenant Wilson, a graduate of the University of Minnesota, was stationed at the Mountain Home Air Force base. In college his fraternity was Beta Theta Pi and he also belonged to Gray Friars, men's honorary.

Following their marriage the lieutenant and his bride will make their home in Great Falls, Mont. • • •

TOP: After living in Montana for a while, the newlyweds moved to Minneapolis. MIDDLE: Rosie's newspaper wedding announcement. MIDDLE RIGHT: Rosie's college photo. LOWER: Rosie (upper right) volunteering at a youth camp in college.

TOP LEFT: Gerry at the DMZ in Korea. TOP RIGHT: Gerry at a Korean orphanage. BOTTOM: Gerry (upper right) in Korea serving as a lieutenant in the personnel department (this photo was taken for the squadron's yearbook).

AN AMERICAN FAMILY

1955

One year after Gerry left for Korea, Rosie stood with a crowd on a San Francisco pier. Exuberant wives and children waved and held up signs while a military band played. In front of them, a colossal troopship overflowed with service members. Anxiously, Rosie scanned the faces on board.

At last, there he was!

Spotting Gerry on the top deck, Rosie beamed with joy. A few moments later, he walked down the gangplank just a hundred feet in front of her. She desperately wanted to go to him, but a three-foot makeshift barrier blocked her way, and a young serviceman stood guard. As Rosie saw her husband getting closer, she thought, *There's no way that kid is going to stop me!*

Rosie started to climb over the barrier. "Hey, lady, you can't go in there!" the guard shouted. But before he could stop her, she hopped over it and sprinted toward Gerry. They collided at the base of the ramp in a joyful embrace.

They spent several days in San Francisco, then drove to Mazatlán, Mexico for a second honeymoon. Afterward, they enjoyed the long drive north to Minnesota to begin their new life together. As Gerry puts it, "I was fresh out of the military, married, tan, and happy. I needed only one thing now—a job."

Gerry and Rosie moved to Minneapolis and rented a bungalow. Their furniture consisted of a mattress on the floor and canvas butterfly chairs. But it was home; they both felt they had died and gone to heaven. They needed to get Minnesota license plates for their car, so they went to the local bank to cash a check. After the transaction, the bank manager asked Gerry, "What do you do for work?"

"I just returned from Korea."

After an impromptu interview, the manager promptly offered Gerry a job at the bank.

In his new position, Gerry often worked at the bond

TOP: 1968 Christmas photo with Sadie the dog and Mathilda the cat. LEFT TO RIGHT: Libby, Rosie Bill, Mick, Gerry, Katy. RIGHT PAGE: BOTTOM LEFT: Gerry and Rosie with their newly adopted daughter Katy and Prudence the dog in 1961.

desk. Every Friday, a quiet and unassuming customer would come and buy a savings bond for his mother. His name was Charles Shultz, the author of *Peanuts*.

Gerry's salary of $275 a month wasn't quite enough to make ends meet, so Rosie took a position as a home economist at Northern States Power. The 1950s were an era of rapid change, and American homeowners were sometimes baffled by all the innovative technology—especially the new home appliances. As a home economist, Rosie drove her company car to area homes and helped residents learn how to use their new electric devices. She also consulted with architects to help them incorporate the updated equipment more efficiently. And, because she was a whiz in the kitchen, she held large cooking classes all over Minneapolis. Soon Rosie was making more money than Gerry—an anomaly in that day. But Gerry didn't mind. Their dual income enabled them to buy a simple home in Bloomington, a suburb of Minneapolis.

In 1958 Gerry left banking and became a stockbroker. They moved to Alexandria, just north of Minneapolis, where Gerry began building his clientele. His investing acumen caught the eye of two local television executives who suggested he create a financial show for TV. Soon, Gerry was hosting *The Weekly Business Review*, a seven-minute investing program that aired weekly, just after *Sports and Weather* and before *People are Funny* with Art Linkletter. As a recognized TV personality, he began receiving mail from all over the state. And, of course, his newfound notoriety enhanced his brokerage business.

Meanwhile, Rosie became a media personality in her own right. Building on her popularity as a home economist, she began hosting a radio show. Executives at the same TV station where Gerry worked noticed the popularity of Rosie's radio show, so they invited her to do a weekly live TV cooking show. Rosie was like an early version of Martha Stewart and Julia Child rolled into one. Ironically, Gerry and Rosie didn't own a TV set. But now, with both of them hosting TV shows, they decided it was time to buy one. Gerry was proud of her. He felt her hour-long show, versus his seven-minute segment, made her the real star of the family.

A top-ten national investment firm took over Gerry's brokerage firm and offered him a position in Minneapolis. He and Rosie didn't want to live in a big city, so Gerry accepted the idea of opening a branch office in the small town of Austin, Minnesota, the home of Hormel ("Spam-town"). Their move to Austin began a happy, ten-year period filled with good friends, dinner parties, golf, and barbecues. Gerry's growing business eventually employed six stockbrokers.

But something was missing.

Both Rosie and Gerry wanted children. Rosie envisioned herself as a mother of six. But their diligent efforts to start a family hadn't succeeded. Meanwhile, they were watching their peers grow families, seemingly without any impediments. Finally, after eight frustrating years, they decided to adopt. They went through the lengthy legal process and were overjoyed at last to bring home a ten-month-old girl named Katy.

Ironically, two years after adopting, Rosie gave birth to their first son, Bill. And eighteen months after that she had me, Mick. Then another year later, Libby came along. Looking back now, Rosie says, "Before we adopted her, Katy looked like the poster child for the Minnesota Children's Home Society. Because we now had a little girl, I guess we just relaxed and had three biological children of our own."

Gerry adds, "We really appreciated our children because of all the frustration and time it took to start our family. But now, our cup runneth over."

CALIFORNIA HERE WE COME

1969

Gerry received a call at home one Thursday night from the president of his brokerage firm. He asked Gerry if he'd be willing to relocate to California and manage the firm's West Coast division. He would need to decide soon, as he was expected to report on Monday—three days later. Rosie and Gerry had considered moving to Denver, Colorado, for the skiing, but Southern California was not on their radar. Rosie didn't like the idea of Los Angeles. "I wore out three pairs of shoes dragging my heels," she recalls, "because I didn't want to move to 'the land of the fruits and nuts.'" Rosie called some of the corporate wives she knew who lived in California. They persuaded her that it was a diverse area and a great place to raise a family.

Gerry worked in Los Angeles and flew home two weekends a month. He searched for a community that was close to Los Angeles but had a small-town feel. Back in Minnesota, Rosie arranged for the sale of the home and organized the move. Over the next three months, they talked over the phone daily, and he mailed her photos of various neighborhoods. They finally decided to settle in San Marino, a suburb of Los Angeles. Soon, Gerry piled the family into their green station wagon and drove us across the country with Rosie, four kids, a basset hound named Sadie, and our cat, Mathilda.

TOP: 1969 family Christmas card. MIDDLE PHOTO: Family backpacking in Mammoth Mountain.
BOTTOM PHOTO: Our two dogs, Red and Budweiser, dragging Gerry on a walk on Milan Avenue.

MILAN AVENUE, SOUTH PASADENA

After two years in San Marino, we moved to the adjacent city of South Pasadena. This was a city of 25,000 with one high school and one middle school. There were four little league fields, a single hardware store, one small golf course, a pet shop, two banks, one drug store that sold ten-cent scoops of ice cream, and a historic movie theater called *The Rialto*. Each summer, patriotic residents would line the main street to watch the annual 4th of July Parade. I could almost picture Andy Griffith and Opie participating in that parade. It was that kind of town.

As agreeable as Southern California was, Rosie found the social atmosphere a bit disconnected compared to the Midwest. Instead of complaining, she decided to be the kind of neighbor she would want to have. As Rosie pruned roses in her front yard, she made a point of talking with people passing by. On special occasions, she took homemade desserts with handwritten notes to the neighbors. After about two years, Rosie knew every person and family on the long block. Soon, our street felt like a friendly Midwestern neighborhood.

Our house on Milan Avenue was a large, two-story colonial with a pool, a two-room pool house, and a two-car garage. In the half-acre backyard were two massive oak trees and a giant avocado tree that I often climbed to pick the softball-sized fruits. I'd toss them down to Bill, who caught them in his catcher's glove.

Mature oaks and giant magnolia trees arched high over the street, almost touching in the middle. Tall greenish-copper antique street lanterns accented the sidewalks and large front yards. There were many majestic, older homes—and lots of children. We all played after school

until the street lanterns came on, signaling that it was time to go home for dinner. If we didn't come in, our mom would stand on the front porch with a large Japanese temple bell and ring it with a wooden mallet. The sound could be heard a half-mile away! The street's idyllic ambiance caught the attention of Hollywood filmmakers, who shot numerous movies there, including some in our home. The best part of those events was the catered food, which the film crews opened up to the residents in the neighborhood.

Family dinners were a regular custom for the Wilsons. We'd sometimes gather around our large kitchen table, but we usually ate in the formal dining room so we kids could learn manners. Gerry and Rosie always encouraged discussion and challenged us to look up things in the encyclopedia. On Sundays, Gerry led a home Bible study at the dining table. When we were teenagers, family dinners were where our parents exposed us kids to wine—a little sip here and there. Since our parents treated wine as a normal part of life, it didn't seem like the *forbidden fruit*.

"The Milan House," as many friends called it, gained a reputation for being warm and inviting. On holidays, people without family nearby were invited to our house for dinner. We welcomed teens from troubled homes who longed to experience a healthier family. This extended family grew to include classmates, church friends, business colleagues, international exchange students, neighbors, and out-of-town visitors. Gerry would often call Rosie and say, "I'm bringing two people home for dinner tonight, okay?" And we kids would bring our friends home. Rosie was always happy to set a few more places.

PHOTO: A family dinner in our dining room with friends, relatives and a Brazilian exchange student on right.

"In 12 years, we've never been disappointed in a Cure 81 ham."

MRS. R. G. WILSON,
Pasadena, California

At Hormel, since the very beginning, we've taken the time to inspect and register every Cure /81 ham individually. No other ham you can buy gives you this assurance of dependable leanness, tenderness and flavor. Ham after ham, slice after slice.

It's good to know that makes a difference to you.

Hormel FINE FOOD PRODUCTS

cure 81

REGISTERED BONELESS HAM

Hormel Cure 81 Ham. Dependability worth paying for.

ROSIE THE HAM LADY

Rosie had another opportunity to be on TV when she lived in South Pasadena. When she and Gerry lived in Minnesota in the 1950s, they had a friend who was head of advertising for meats at Hormel (based in Austin, Minnesota). He was aware that Rosie once hosted a popular TV cooking show in Minnesota.

The director flew her to Minneapolis from California to film a commercial for Hormel. They shot about 30 takes and took numerous still pictures. The TV spot had her saying, "You know, in 12 years I've never been disappointed

in Cure 81 ham. Now that's dependability worth paying for." The ads were in *Reader's Digest*, and *Good Housekeeping*, to name just a few.

One day while Gerry was on a business trip in Hawaii, he turned on the TV and there Rosie was, selling Cure 81 ham! He smiled at how beautiful she looked. It is interesting that Rosie went from selling ham to making one a pet.

27   *TOP: An ad that featured Rosie. TOP RIGHT: Rosie in South Pasadena holding a Cure 81 ham. RIGHT PAGE: Rosie and Gerry visiting the South Pasadena home in 2017.*

PETS AND PIGS

The Wilson hospitality wasn't limited to humans either. We welcomed pets of all kinds—refugees from bad homes or strays from the local animal shelter. At one point, we had a pig, five dogs, three cats, a hamster, a parakeet, and a fish. The dogs became the best greeters at our house. Every guest was warmly welcomed at the front door by at least one dog. But our most colorful pet—and eventually the most famous—was Sophie, a potbellied pig we kids gave to Rosie for a Mother's Day present. Two feet long and a foot high, Sophie was cute and smart. She slept and ate inside, and her favorite pastime was cuddling on the couch with the family as we watched TV.

Sophie settled happily into life in the Wilson home. But a grumpy city councilman heard we were harboring a pig in our home (news travels fast in South Pasadena). He didn't want to see his beloved city overrun with cows, pigs, and goats, so he pulled out an eighty-year-old law that prohibited residents from keeping farm animals in South Pasadena. The city informed us that our beloved Sophie had to go.

The ensuing uproar over the potbellied pig became such a hotly-debated issue in town, that it went all the way to the city council. The subsequent meeting, known as *The Ham Hearing,* had onlookers and reporters packed into the council room. Meanwhile, Rosie brought Sophie, dressed in an adorable pink tutu. The *pig problem* was the last agenda item of the evening. Rosie kept Sophie occupied during the lengthy meeting by feeding her green grapes.

When the time came, Rosie walked to the mic and spoke eloquently on Sophie's behalf. During the discussion, the complaining councilman was still adamant in his resistance. The council deliberated for a few more minutes, and then they all voted. Sophie won the day— she could stay! The crowd clapped, and cameras flashed while Sophie continued eating grapes.

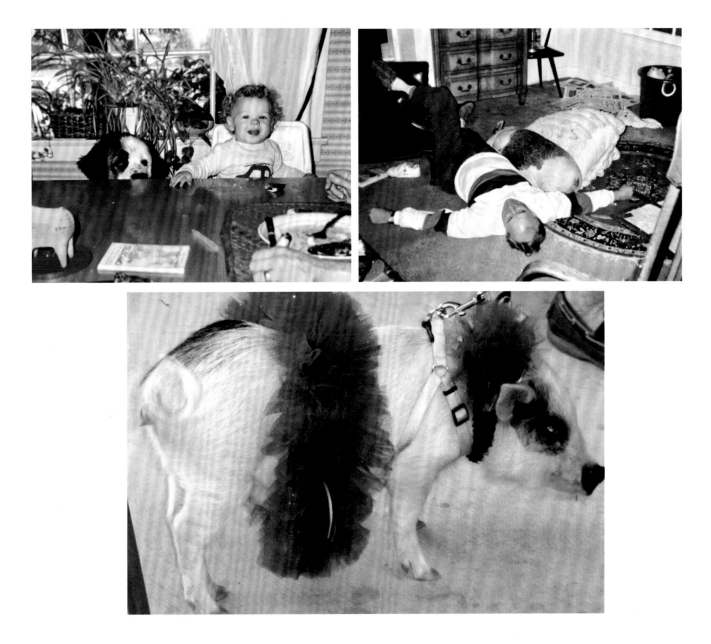

A few days later, a female reporter from the *Los Angeles Times* came to our house for a story. As she interviewed Gerry and Rosie, Sophie began sniffing the reporter's purse. Without warning, our brazen pig plunged her head into the open purse, yanked out some lipstick with her mouth, and sprinted around the house while she devoured her find. When Rosie caught up with the pig, she laughed as she noticed Sophie's lips and mouth caked in red. I guess you can "put lipstick on a pig."

The *LA Times* published an article with the headline, "This Little Piggy Came to South Pasadena—and Stayed." Potbellied pigs were not well-known at that time. But after the piece ran, Rosie received calls from people all over the Los Angeles area wanting to know how they could get a permit for a pet pig. Rosie obliged them, and soon, many

friends came to love the idea of having a potbellied pig of their own. Sophie helped by bearing numerous piglets, all of whom found homes across the region.

Sophie even caught the eye of the actor, Nicolas Cage, who came to our house to film a movie. Years later, while working as a flight attendant, Libby ran into him on a plane. "You might not remember," she said, "but you filmed a scene at our house in South Pasadena."

His face instantly lit up. "Ah, yes," he said. "You were the colonial house—the family with the cute pig wearing a pink tutu!"

The city eventually updated its old law about farm animals. And the pot-bellied pig trend continued to grow. As far as we know, it started—at least in part—in South Pasadena, on Milan Avenue.

LEFT PAGE: TOP: Rosie entertaining the neighbor kids in the front yard with Sophie the pig. Libby and Heather on the left. BOTTOM LEFT TO RIGHT: Budweiser investigating the new family pig. Gerry in the backyard wearing a kimono given to him by our exchange students from Japan. Sophie eating after she fed her piglets in our den. RIGHT PAGE: TOP: Budweiser, our St. Bernard, intently eying a piece of pizza crust in front of Christopher. TOP RIGHT: Gerry stretching on our den floor with Sophie nuzzling up to him. BOTTOM: Sophie dressed for the "The Ham Hearing."

FAMOUS WILSON PARTIES

South Pasadena didn't have a place for young people to hang out, so our home became the teen center our quiet city needed. We hosted graduation parties, church parties, booster club parties, and team parties. The attendance would range from 20 to over 400. Local teens would often drive by Milan Avenue to see if something was going on at the Wilson house. If they saw more than two cars parked, they'd walk down the driveway to see what was happening. As a family, we had a deal— no parties without Rosie and Gerry present. I think they both had as much fun as we kids did. And Rosie, especially, felt we were doing a service for the community by providing a safe place for teens to have fun.

For the neighbors' sake, we always made sure the noise stopped by 10:00 p.m. All the neighbors were okay with

that—except for one, who *always* called the police. We began taking bets on what time the police would arrive. Most of the time, the police were very cooperative since they knew our family and what my folks were trying to do for the local youth.

But at one giant party of 250 teens, two officers rolled up at 9:00 p.m. with their squad car lights flashing. One of the officers was fresh out of the police academy and new to South Pasadena. He marched up the brick path toward Rosie, who stood on the porch with her arms crossed. "We received an angry complaint," he announced. "I demand that you shut the party down *now!*"

Gerry was in the backyard keeping an eye on things as he trusted Rosie to handle the police. Numerous students went to the front yard as they heard the police were there. Rosie took a breath. "Everything is under control, and I will personally make sure the music is turned down at 10:00 as we've promised to all the neighbors."

"No, I said, *shut it down—now!*" the newbie blurted.

Rosie's voice took on a stern-teacher tone. "I understand your concern, but we are hosting all these kids, and they are having a fun time. We have always turned it down, and it has worked out every time."

The young officer's eyes opened wide. He leaned back a bit and stared hard at Rosie. "If you do not shut this party down this second, I will be forced to handcuff someone and take them to the station!"

By now, a dozen young people were looking on, awaiting the next move. Rosie looked the young officer in the eye and declared, "If you need to arrest someone, then cuff *me* right now!"

At that moment, the senior officer stepped in. "No, Mrs. Wilson," he said, "we can't arrest *you.*"

Rosie walked down the brick steps and stood in front of the officers. Extending both arms toward the younger officer as though she were surrendering to arrest, she said, "Then either handcuff me right now or kindly leave!"

The senior officer intervened again. "That won't be necessary, Mrs. Wilson," he said. "Please keep the music down and close the party by 10:00 p.m. We'll deal with the neighbor. Have a nice evening."

The officers got back in their squad car, turned off their flashing lights, and drove away. Rosie turned around and walked back inside. The onlookers all stood in quiet amazement, then a few people started clapping. The story of Rosie's legendary standoff spread throughout the entire party in approximately 2.5 minutes.

LEFT PAGE: TOP: On the front steps of our home, 1982. BOTTOM: Katy's wedding and reception in our backyard. Rosie and Gerry are on the left in the reception line. RIGHT PAGE: TOP: Family photo in 1979 with friend, Anthony, who stayed with us for three years. Mick and Bill were rockin' the corduroy suits. BOTTOM: Friends from the class of 1981 on the dance floor (basketball area in front of our garage) at one of our large parties.

KATY

In 1980 Katy married her long-time boyfriend in the Milan Avenue backyard on the hottest day of the summer. We threw a large reception in our backyard, and Rosie cooked for 200 people. As the party died down around 10:00 p.m. Rosie went into the kitchen to finish the dishes. An hour later, she reappeared outside, exhausted. Her blue linen suit was caked with food scraps and frosting. After chatting with some of the 75 remaining guests, she walked over to the swimming pool. She retreated about six steps, turned back toward the water, sprinted, and jumped, fully clothed, into the deep end with a loud "Woo-hoo!"

There were a few seconds of stunned silence—and then everyone cheered.

Within three years after her wedding, Katy gave birth to two beautiful children, Heather and Christopher. But her story took a sad turn. Since middle school, Katy had wrestled with drugs. We hoped her life would turn around after marriage and kids, but her issues continued. It became apparent to our family that she was incapable of being a responsible parent.

Gerry and Rosie decided to intervene; they took temporary custody of Katy's two children, Heather (three years old) and Christopher (six weeks old). When Katy didn't improve, my folks decided to take the next step and adopt. Gerry and Rosie were both 57 years old.

As Gerry puts it, "With adoption, I can now say, 'That's my son! That's my daughter.' Adoption is almost *more* than blood because you chose them. It is a heartfelt act, saying, 'I want you.' My view of adoption is this: once you're adopted, you are blood. Society says, 'Blood is thicker than water.' It's keeping people separate somehow. But we've decided to be together, so once we've done that, you are blood."

After the long adoption process, Rosie and Gerry—now almost 60 years-old and having raised four kids—were told they must take parenting classes. They chuckled but dutifully did so.

And Rosie? She felt God had finally given her the six children she always wanted.

EMPTY HOUSE

One by one, the Wilson kids moved out and scattered all over California. Gerry and Rosie considered downsizing and moving to a quiet area, as many of their friends had done, but the sedentary life was not for them.

Libby graduated from Long Beach State with honors. She worked as a flight attendant then married Craig in 1995. They lived in the Central Coast wine country in Solvang. In his job as a golf pro, Craig met numerous retired executives and winery owners. He thought the kind of lives these people enjoyed would be ideal for Rosie and Gerry. So Libby and Craig discussed the idea with them, and immediately Gerry liked the thought of downsizing and lowering his golf handicap. Plus, Craig considered, if the folks bought property in one of the many vineyards there, the sales of grapes could help sustain their new life as adoptive parents.

I worked in banking for a few years after graduating from the University of Colorado in 1986. Then, I enrolled at Fuller Theological Seminary and earned a Master of Divinity degree. Afterward, a colleague and I started a church in Pasadena. Our goal was to build a "church for the unchurched." To pay the bills, I worked as a substitute teacher at the local high schools and part-time with Bill in estate planning.

Bill was a quarterback at Pasadena City College and then at Weber State University in Ogden, Utah. After graduating with a business degree, he moved back to California and rented an apartment in the San Diego suburb of Pacific Beach, where he met Jenifer. They married and moved to Mission Viejo in Orange County. Soon they had two beautiful daughters, Cassidy and Cambria. Bill made a living selling annuities and mutual funds but found that he despised the routine of cold-calling for potential clients. In the early 1990s, Bill decided to start a mergers and acquisitions company, partnering with an eccentric financial analyst who had some experience in the field.

Gerry dipped into his retirement funds to provide startup money and convinced a long-time friend to invest as well. But things didn't go as planned. Over the next 18 months, the new company couldn't close a single deal. Bill and his business partner closed their doors, and all the investors lost their money.

Bill wrestled with the failure of the company, his career, and his life's purpose. By all appearances, he'd been living the American dream—a lovely home in Orange County, a beautiful wife, and two amazing daughters. But his heart yearned for something more in his career—anything that would help him regain his passion and purpose.

LEFT PAGE: TOP: Heather and Christopher. BOTTOM: Family with Rick, our Swedish exchange student. RIGHT PAGE: TOP LEFT: Mick and Bill were both presidents of the Beta Theta Pi Fraternity chapters at their respective colleges. Mick was president at University of Colorado at Boulder, and Bill at Weber State University in Utah. Gerry was also president of his Beta chapter at the University of Minnesota. TOP RIGHT: Bill in the financial world. BOTTOM LEFT: Craig and Libby at their wedding in Foxborough, Mass. Heather is to Craig's left along with other nieces and nephews. Mick officiated. BOTTOM RIGHT: Libby in her American Airlines flight attendant uniform with her brothers.

Cabernet Hill →

PART TWO:
THE DAWN OF A WINERY

2019

THE CALL

"I'm beyond frustrated! Nothing in business seems to click. I feel like I'm adrift, and I've lost my passion."

Bill was confiding in his good friend, Steve, who had been the best man at his wedding. It was 1995, and Bill felt disenchanted with life in the financial world. "What do you think I should do?"

Steve didn't miss a beat. "I know exactly what you should do," he said. "I just got back from wine tasting in Temecula. There's a small winery for sale there, and the owner is 74 years old, single, no kids. He's tired and wants out. I immediately thought of you and the whole Wilson family. He'd even be willing to help finance the sale." Steve felt that Bill and the Wilsons could make this winery successful.

Bill quickly saw the potential in this unexpected opportunity. He hung up and thought, *This is it! It's perfect! I could do this. We could do this.* Running a winery felt like the new direction he'd been desiring. He discussed it with Jenifer. She agreed it was worth pursuing. Now all he had to do was convince the rest of the family. He started by calling our parents.

Rosie picked up the phone, and Bill blurted out, "Hey, do you want to buy a winery?"

"You're crazy," she said with a laugh. "We've never made wine!"

"But you made rhubarb and dandelion wine in your basement in Minnesota."

Rosie chuckled. "I don't think making wine in new garbage pails qualifies us."

Bill pushed on with his best sales pitch. "Think of it as a family project."

"I still think you're crazy, but let me put Gerry on the phone."

Gerry heard Bill's idea and said, "Wow, you are crazy—but this sounds like fun! What does the rest of the family say?"

To Bill, that was like a green light. "I'll find out," he said.

When Bill called me, I was in the middle of starting a church in Pasadena. He knew I was committed to ministry work, so I might be the hardest to convince. He broached the idea of our family entering the winemaking business.

"Well," I said, "making wine *was* Jesus' first miracle."

I could almost see him smiling over the phone. "Hey, bro," he continued, "Let's do this! It's a chance for the family to come together again. You can split time between the church and helping fix up the winery!"

"It sounds like fun. Let's check it out."

Next, Bill called Libby and Craig in Solvang. She responded, "Where is Temecula?"

Most of us were only vaguely familiar with this growing community in Southwest Riverside County. But we all found the idea of running a winery intriguing. Our family had always enjoyed good wine and would often visit winery tasting rooms. On one visit to a winery in Paso Robles, we all met the owners who gave us a personal tour. We witnessed the pressing of the grapes and tasted wine straight out of the barrel. Afterward, we regrouped in the parking lot and talked about what we had just experienced. Someone said, "Wouldn't this be fun for us to do together someday?"

Now, it suddenly seemed like a real possibility.

The family members gathered at the Wilson home in South Pasadena to discuss the idea.

Libby liked the thought of being close to Rosie and Gerry in their later years. Craig loved the idea of working in the wine business. I envisioned the family reconnecting and experiencing that vibe we had growing up in South Pasadena. Bill needed a new start for himself and his family. Jenifer thought living in the country would be fun for her girls. She also knew Bill needed a drastic change. Rosie and Gerry hoped the family could reunite and work together. They also felt Temecula would be an excellent place to raise their newly adopted children, Chris and Heather. It was looking like a yes, all the way around. A week later, Bill called the family members and said, "Let's all go and investigate this winery! I already arranged a tour with the owner."

We had no idea what we were getting into.

37   *The original Cabernet vines located next to Creekside Grille during winter dormancy. These vines were planted in 1969.*

The next week we all met at Bill's house in Mission Viejo, packed into his Suburban, and drove an hour to Temecula. We pulled into the winery at noon. The empty gravel lot had eight parking spaces marked off with railroad ties. The winery's tasting room was a modest, one-story, beige, stucco building with a long wooden front porch lined with old wine barrels. Behind the building sat a boxy-looking metal warehouse filled with a few wine tanks and pallets of wine. An old tractor, a rusted wine press, and some other beat-up wine equipment sat idly in the space between the two buildings. The restroom facilities consisted of a single Porta-Potty.

Behind the winery buildings, rolling hills laden with orange and golden grapevines shimmered in the autumn sunlight. A lone gravel road cut through the middle of the vineyard to a large Spanish-style home on the hill.

We walked inside the tasting room, where a solitary employee was cleaning wine glasses. Wine bottles and gift shop items cluttered the tasting room which made it feel like an old antique store. Bill and I started to brainstorm on how we could fix it up: redesign the tasting bar, add a better seating area, build indoor restrooms, install some

windows to bring in more natural light and upgrade the landscaping. Excitement built as we thought about the potential of this property. After about 15 minutes we all met the owner who showed us the rest of the grounds, including the large home on the hill just above the winery.

After the tour, we all thanked the owner, and gathered as a family in the parking lot to debrief. The property needed a ton of work, but we all loved the quaint winery and surrounding vineyards. We began to believe that, together, we could pull this off.

In the weeks following, Bill and Gerry came down a few more times and began negotiations with the owner. They both called him often to finalize the details of the sale. However, after a month the owner became less responsive to their calls and questions.

Rosie and Gerry decided to visit the winery unannounced after a wedding they attended in Temecula. They walked into the tasting room and saw the owner laughing and sipping wine with two pretty young women. "Ah," he said, "the Wilsons are here! Come on in!"

Rosie recalls, "I looked to Gerry and quietly said, 'He doesn't want to sell!' I knew why the owner was not

INVESTIGATING TEMECULA

moving these negotiations forward. I think he initially believed he wanted to sell. But that winery was his social life, and I think it was hard for him to walk away from what he knew so well. We were cordial for an awkward five minutes, and then we left."

However, over the next two weeks, the owner seemed to show a renewed interest in the deal. He talked with Bill and Gerry on the phone to work on the details. As a family we were excited to see the negotiations progressing. The owner set a date for us to come to Temecula to discuss the final terms of the sale. Maybe this was the day our family would own a winery! Bill and Gerry drove to Temecula to meet with the owner and his attorney in the lawyer's office.

"We sat down," Bill recalls, "and the owner said he was still open to selling the winery. We asked what exactly the selling price included. He told us that another winemaker owned all the fermentation tanks. He then listed all the additional equipment that was not included in the price, such as wine filters, grape presses, and pumps. He also told us the deal required us to purchase the 1,000 cases of his own labeled wine that he had stored at the win-

ery. To comply with the current building codes, he said we'd need to build accessibility for the disabled, widen the road for the entrance, and install fire hydrants and sprinkler systems. The $850,000 initial price tag grew to $1,400,000. I wish the owner had let us know this earlier. This whole meeting ticked me off."

Bill and Gerry knew we couldn't afford the higher amount. They thanked the owner and his attorney and walked to Bill's Suburban. They sat in the parking lot dumbfounded. "Bill and I were dismayed," Gerry recalls. "We both knew that winery was no longer a fit for us—the new deal wasn't worth it. 'Where do we go from here?' Bill asked. We drove off, discouraged, and discussed other options."

A week later, the whole family gathered at the South Pasadena house to discuss our future. Do we look for another winery to purchase? Do we give up on the idea altogether and continue with our separate lives?

TEMECULA FUN FACTS

• The first vines were planted by Spanish padres in the late 1700s from grapevines they brought from Spain. In the late 1800s, acres of vines were planted on the Pechanga Reservation (Wilson Creek manages some of those old vines today).

• **Stagecoach:** In 1858 Temecula became a stop for the Butterfield Overland Stage route. In 1859, the Temecula Post Office was the first post office in inland Southern California.

• **First commercial vineyard:** 1968, Audrey and Vincenzo Cilurzo

• **First commercial winery:** Callaway Winery, 1971

• Temecula Valley is a recognized American Viticultural Area (AVA) since 1984, comprised of over 30,000 acres. Approximately 2,500 acres are currently used for grape growing.

• The city of Temecula was incorporated in 1989. The previous name of the area was Rancho California.

• **Name:** Temecula is a Luiseño Indian word meaning "place of the sun." The Spanish translated the word to mean, "where the sun breaks through the mist."

• **Wineries:** 1984: Eight wineries were in operation. In 1996 Wilson Creek was the 14th. Today there are over 45 wineries with ten more in the planning stages.

• **Temecula Population:** 1970: approximately 200; 1980: 4,100; 2000: 30,617; 2019: 114,000

• **Visitors:** 3.1 million people visited Temecula Valley in 2018.

• **Location:** 90 minutes from Los Angeles; 60 minutes from San Diego, Orange County, Riverside, and Palm Springs.

• **Elevation:** 1,500 feet.

• **Ocean influence:** The Pacific Ocean is 22 miles away separated by a mountain range. The ocean breeze comes into Temecula Valley through a gap in the mountains called the *Rainbow Gap.*

• **Temecula Valley Balloon and Wine Festival:** started in 1983. Today it draws over 50,000 attendees to the event at Lake Skinner every year.

• **Temecula Valley** was named one of the 10 best wine travel destinations of 2019 by *Wine Enthusiast Magazine.*

TOP: Entry gate sign into Old Town Temecula. LEFT: Rosie and Gerry visited Temecula in the 1980s for business and golf. RIGHT: Visiting the vineyard property in 1996.

PLAN B

Bill recalls, "We decided to see if there were any other wineries that might be for sale in California. I did an online search for any affordable winery in the state, which I soon learned was an oxymoron; no winery for sale seemed affordable. Over the next few weeks, we ended up refocusing on Temecula. It was close to San Diego and Los Angeles where we could also enjoy the amenities of a large city—the art, the concerts. It could be a beautiful place to raise our families."

A month after the small winery deal fell through, Bill drove to Temecula to meet with a realtor and look at an existing vineyard. She met him at a vineyard property two miles past the last winery on Rancho California Road. They met on a gravel road adjacent to the parcel, overlooking the acres of vines. The realtor pointed out an area where we might build a tasting room. "I couldn't envision what she described," Bill says. "I liked the land and the view, but I couldn't see this vineyard as the place for our winery and homes. As we walked into the vineyard, it was quite funny seeing this blonde realtor making her way through the vines in heels." They spent ten minutes

touring the property. Bill concluded that the parcel was not a fit, as the land was too remote, and he didn't see any place suitable to build a winery.

A few weeks later, a friend referred us to another realtor named Nancy Hughes. Nancy had a reputation as a powerhouse agent who got things done for her clients. Bill called her, and they established an immediate rapport. But she wanted to show him the same property we'd already seen on Rancho California Road. "No way," Bill said. "That property won't work. Another agent showed it to me already."

"Let's look at it again," Nancy replied. "I think you need to see it from a different perspective." Bill reluctantly agreed.

On a beautiful, seventy-degree winter day, Rosie, Gerry, and Bill drove down to see the property again. They turned into the vineyard area and met Nancy. Bill noticed that Nancy wore professional but comfortable shoes conducive to the dirt—a sign of a prepared realtor.

*"That property won't work.
Another agent showed
it to me already."*

*"Let's look at it again.
I think you need to see it from a
different perspective."*

LEFT PAGE: TOP: *Rosie talking with neighbors.* BOTTOM: *Nancy Hughes, pictured here with Gerry in 2010, remains a close family friend.* RIGHT PAGE: *Family visiting the property in 1996.*

Rosie still wrestled with the nagging issue of the property's location nestled seven miles from the freeway and two miles beyond the last winery. Other winery owners told us we'd probably fail within a few years as it was too remote. But it seemed to be the only promising option—old, lime-green toilet and all.

The following week, the whole family came and looked at the property. A week later, we convened at the South Pasadena house to discuss our options. Everyone loved the hilly vineyard with its gnarled, established vines. Bill envisioned the property with a tasting room, production area, home on the hill, and a beautified creek area—ideal for picnicking.

We were also aware of the downsides: we would need to rip out a dozen rows of vines to build the winery from scratch. The property had no existing infrastructure (electrical, septic, phone, hydrants, etc.), and the road needed to be widened to add an entrance/exit lane. Plus, we were a family from the suburbs and had never done anything like this.

The first obstacle was the sheer size of the parcel. At 126 acres, it was too large and pricey for us. Nancy stepped in to help negotiate. The land was owned by

Rosie recalls her first impression:

"Nancy led us through the rolling acres of established vines. We stopped at an overlook on a hill in the middle of the property where we could get a 360-degree view. I liked the mountain views and rustic feel to the land. As we continued touring the grounds, Nancy mentioned that the vineyard was mature—planted in 1969 and 1970. She also mentioned that a woman oversaw the planting process. I liked that a woman's touch was part of the vineyard's history.

We walked down to a lower area by Rancho California Road and saw what appeared to be an illegal dumpsite. As we walked around the overgrown area, we saw old mattresses, rusted water heaters, torn couches, and even an old, broken toilet sitting straight up. Nancy walked us through the brush and trash to a natural creek with large, native willows and spruce trees on both sides. She pointed out that this was the only winery in Southern California with a creek running through the property. Bill liked that fact. She walked us to where we could build an entrance from the road and pointed out where some vines could be removed to build the tasting room. We began to see how this property could work for us. Was this the place for our dream? Maybe."

an Iraqi family that had fled to America when Saddam Hussein came to power. They were shipping the grapes to Napa but were not happy with the return on the sale. They were willing to split off 20 acres, including the area bordering Rancho California Road and the creek. We thought we might be able to swing a purchase of 20 acres, but no more.

There were dozens of unanswered questions and concerns. I asked how we would design and build an entire winery. Craig and Libby were concerned that we were buying just a vineyard and not a working winery. No one had a clue how much it would cost to build a winery. Gerry repeated his vision for a family enterprise that could endure for generations. Bill knew we could make it work, as long as we stayed together. We discussed hiring an architect and builder, which put my mind more at ease. We did a basic calculation on the overall cost, including building the tasting room, creating an entrance from the road, and installing all the required infrastructure. We again felt that, together, we could make it happen.

With a mixture of trepidation and excitement, we all gave it the thumbs up and bought the 20-acre parcel in June 1996. As Bill says, "We were 100 percent in, and you have to watch out when you have 100 percent buy-in with the Wilson Family. When we do something, we go for it. This decision could be the greatest thing for our entire family—or the absolute worst."

Looking back at this time in our history, Gerry recalls, "Why do I think the first winery didn't work out? When that owner backed out, we were initially disappointed. But to this day, we thank that owner for not selling to us. The owner later told me his winery probably wasn't a good idea for our family anyway. We would've likely been a failure, as that winery wasn't big enough for four families to be involved. I believe in God, and I believe this was divine intervention, or whatever you want to call it. We all agree, in retrospect, that God had a better plan for our family."

46

LEFT PAGE: TOP: The natural creek running through the property.
BOTTOM: The creek bed area looking from Rancho California Rd. RIGHT PAGE: Sunset in 2020.

WE NEED A NAME

But now we had to name this winery. We posted a sheet of paper on our folks' refrigerator in South Pasadena so friends and neighbors who visited could write down their ideas. We collected the brainstorms, and then the whole family gathered at Gerry and Rosie's home to discuss.

"How about *Raymond Winery?*" I suggested. Raymond was Gerry's middle name. But we soon found out another winery owned the brand.

"What about *Elizabeth Estates?*" Libby joked. Her full name is Elizabeth.

"How about *Rosemary's Estates?*" someone said. Yes, it would honor Rosie. But we didn't want to name the place after one person; this was a family winery.

Wilson Estates made our list, as well as *Wilson Family Winery.* But that too was taken.

A week later, Bill was driving back from a meeting in Palm Springs. As he entered the Temecula area, he noticed a sign that read, "Wilson Valley." *Could this be our name?* Soon after, he met with the family at South Pasadena and showed us the location on a Thomas Guide map. As he pointed to the map, he noticed that there was a creek running right through Wilson Valley that emptied into Vail Lake. Its name was Wilson Creek.

Bill's eyes opened wide. "Wilson Creek. That's it!" The name immediately clicked for everyone.

With an ear-to-ear smile, Bill said, "Remember what Nancy, our real estate agent said that the natural creek on our property is our difference-maker?"

Even though the actual Wilson Creek was seven miles away from our vineyard property, we unanimously chose the name for our winery, and the creek running through it.

The name wasn't too formal or cliché. At first, Gerry wrestled with the idea of using *Wilson* in the title. He felt it was too pretentious and a bit egocentric. But after looking at many of the winery names in Napa, Sonoma, and Temecula, we realized it was a common practice. Plus, we were a family; why not have our family name for the winery?

Soon after we bought the vineyard land in 1996, a reporter from *The Press-Enterprise* newspaper called to ask Gerry for an interview. The economy was emerging from a recession, and the editors wanted an article highlighting a new family business in the area. Gerry felt we were too new to provide a story but reluctantly agreed. He met with the reporter at a Temecula restaurant.

"You've bet everything on this, haven't you?" the reporter asked.

"Yeah, I guess," Gerry chuckled. "That does sound kind of scary, the way you put it."

"If this winery fails, what is your exit strategy?"

"If it goes under," Gerry joked, "I guess I can be a greeter at Walmart, and I have my Social Security."

That article, "Future looks bright for wine country," appeared in *The Press-Enterprise*, June 1996. Here is an excerpt:

Gerald and Rosie Wilson gave up retirement and their colonial home in South Pasadena for a chance to build a winery in the rolling green hills east of Temecula.

Now they're living their dream, researching the wine business, meeting with architects and builders, and working with their son, Bill, who will manage Wilson Creek Winery, which they hope to have up and running on a 20-acre site later this year, after the summer harvest.

"He gets so enthusiastic about it I can't stop him from talking about it," Bill Wilson said of his father, a retired financial advisor with a deep, soothing voice who prefers that family members and friends call him "Ger."

Both father and son know enough about the wine business to realize that wineries are capital-intensive enterprises that are subject to the vagaries of nature and people's palates.

The article also included Gerry's Walmart comment. Four years later, Gerry and Rosie were signing wine bottles at the Temecula Walmart during the holidays. The general manager approached Gerry and said with a sly smile, "Gerry, do you remember the Walmart comment you made in that article years ago? I want you to know, you will always have a job at Walmart, any time you want."

LEFT PAGE: TOP LEFT: Bill brainstorming how to build a bridge as a large tractor grades the pad for the winery.
TOP RIGHT: Gerry, Bill and Christopher chatting with local vineyard manager, Ben Drake. The Mazda minivan was our workhorse in transporting debris to the dump. BOTTOM: Gerry talking with Heather near our first structure, the pig house we brought from South Pasadena. RIGHT PAGE: Bill with Jenifer's family and Rosie in the lower garden after a long day of clearing debris. The big pot of chili was, of course, prepared by Rosie.

MOVING AND MOVING AND MOVING

In 1996, Gerry and Rosie put their house up for sale in South Pasadena. It sold in one day. They planned to build a custom home on the 20-acre vineyard. We all worked together around the kitchen table in South Pasadena to design a two-story Italian villa that would be on top of the hill, above the winery. We had a local architect do some preliminary blueprints. While the home was being designed and built, they would need to rent.

They soon found an affordable rental in Temecula. It was a month-to-month rate as the owner left the chance open that she might want to sell the home. If it sold, Rosie and Gerry might have to move with only 30 days' notice. But the price was right. However, after six months in their rental home, they got the notice that they needed to move. They soon found another house with the same "lower rate, no guarantee" agreement. That house sold within a month. So, Bill and I packed them up and moved them to their third rental home. That made three moves in under two years. One friend of Rosie's jokingly told Rosie, "If I need to sell my house, can I rent it to you first?"

RIGHT PAGE: TOP: Bill and Mick during one of the three moves Rosie and Gerry had to make. BOTTOM RIGHT: Gerry and Rosie going over blueprints of their two-story Italian villa they planned to build on the hill above the winery.

OPERATION CLEAN-UP

Our first task after buying the property was to begin the massive cleanup. The rolling hills with their elegant vines looked beautiful, but the areas adjacent to the creek and Rancho California Road were a heap of trash, overgrown trees, and thick shrubbery. The previous owners were absentee landlords, so the property was unsupervised. Many outsiders took advantage of this by using it as an illegal dumping ground rather than traveling 30 minutes to the actual dumpsite.

The whole family started cleaning up the overgrown creek bed. No one in the family had a truck, so at first, we used the family's Mazda minivan with a 5'x7' open-bed trailer we bought used. Over the next two months, we made about 20 trips to the dumpsite, which was 25 miles away in Lake Elsinore.

We also had to deal with a massive, open trench on a dirt road that cut through the vineyard. Over the years, the rain runoff from the vines had carved a small canyon through the road. It was 75 feet long, 12 feet deep and 10 feet wide—so big that the vehicles would drive to the side of it. At its bottom were old dishwashers, wooden

pallets, sinks, and a rusted diesel truck engine. We found a neighbor with a backhoe tractor who helped us clear it out and then fill it with dirt.

Once we cleaned out the creek area, we paid a friend with a large Caterpillar D-8 tractor to level the uneven ground near the creek. But the driver went too close to the water and got the massive tractor stuck in the mud. The 40-ton machine sank halfway into the muck as if it were quicksand. The driver waited until the afternoon sun warmed the ground up and, thankfully, was able to deftly wiggle it out with the help of another tractor.

It took us more than three months, but the creek-bed area was finally looking better. We began calling it, somewhat optimistically, the *lower garden*. We spent more time thinning the overgrowth of cattails in the pond. Bill and I built some wood-chip walkways and we brought in shrubs and leftover flowers from local wholesale nurseries. I made a simple wooden bridge to span the creek. Meanwhile, Jenifer installed a large rope swing on a tree, which her two young girls and many neighbor kids enjoyed. We also bought some cheap lawn furniture so we could relax and enjoy some wine or a cold beer after a long day's work.

LEFT PAGE: Merlot taking a break while Rosie plants flowers by the creek. RIGHT PAGE: TOP: Bill on a borrowed tractor with Rosie in the background. BOTTOM LEFT TO RIGHT: Jenifer and Cambria in the lower garden. Christopher (upper right) building a tree fort with friends. Mick building a basic bridge while Taffy scopes out a squirrel.

One by one, each family moved to Temecula. A few months after Gerry and Rosie's move, Craig and Libby moved to Temecula from Solvang in July 1996.

Meanwhile, Bill's heart was divided between two worlds—his finance business and the winery. He tried working at both for several months, but increasingly found himself pulled toward the winery. A wise mentor told Bill that he was an entrepreneur at heart, and his job in financial planning was draining him. He advised Bill to leave sales and pursue his growing passion—the winery.

Bill and Jenifer discussed moving to Temecula. In early 1997 they went all-in. They sold their home in Mission Viejo and bought a used, double-wide mobile home in Temecula. They parked their new home in the vineyard 200 feet from the future winery building. The plan was that this mobile home would be temporary until they could build their permanent residence on the second floor of the winery a year later.

Bill and Jenifer moved in August—the hottest month of the year. During those first few weeks, they had no electricity or running water and no refrigerator. It was like camping, but without the s'mores. They rented a beat-up Porta-Potty and used a portable generator for power. Bill hooked up a garden hose to the vineyard water system for drinking water and outdoor showers.

They thought this camping phase would last a couple of weeks. Instead, it lasted over two months.

Jenifer recalls the anxiety their move produced: "There were a lot of skeptics on my end—my family and friends who said, 'Are you really going to sell everything, get rid of your house and everything you have and just throw it all into this winery that you have no experience in building or running?' They thought we were completely crazy!"

As Jenifer admits, they had a point: "We probably were too risky, looking back on it now. At that time, my girls were one and three years old, and we lived in a nice comfortable house in Mission Viejo that was in a good area with friendly neighbors. We were going to move onto the vineyard property, and my friends and family had never heard of Temecula."

They soon discovered there were other residents in their new surroundings—of the rodent variety. The land had never had a structure on it, only vines. So, when the double-wide went in, the mice thought Bill had built them their own *Habitrail.* Mice, rats, and all their droppings were everywhere.

One hot August day, Jenifer, Bill, and the girls went to Gerry and Rosie's house to join Libby and Craig in celebrating the folks' 50th anniversary. When they left the double-wide, they inadvertently left the sliding door slightly open. When they returned and switched the lights on, they witnessed dozens of mice and rats scampering on the floor and counters. The rodents had come in from the heat and turned Bill and Jenifer's home into their party.

After a few weeks of persistent heat and ever-present mice, Jenifer began having second thoughts:

DESIGNING THE WINERY

"I became irritable and moody. I thought, what am I doing? I shouldn't be doing this! We should never have done this! This new venture isn't going to work out. Oh man, I should have stayed in my comfortable house! We were living amongst coyotes, snakes, rabbits, and rodents running all over the place. I seriously felt like we were living in the Green Acres TV show. We crossed our fingers and prayed a lot that this whole thing would work out. I stuck with it for the love of my husband. We had a vision and a desire to make it happen. Very quickly, this winery had become our dream and passion. We had sold our house, and we were all in. Where else would we go, and what else would we do?"

Bill started making plans for the tasting room and production area. He had to learn quickly about septic systems, fire hydrant installation, electrical requirements, backflow and irrigation systems, vineyard management, turn lanes, building codes, handicap laws, and water treatment. Bill researched as much as he could. We were shocked at how much it took to put a spade in the ground. Other wineries warned us that it would cost us at least $100,000 just for the county fees. They underestimated. There was a fee to examine the endangered kangaroo rat, and another payment to the Department of Fish and Game to research the creek area. We had to pay transportation fees, a school fee, a water drainage study fee, a soil testing fee, and flood control fees.

Gerry's retirement money was enough for a down payment on the land, but not enough to build a tasting room

and all the needed infrastructure. We needed a construction loan. Gerry and Bill wrote a business plan that projected 250 guests per week and 5,000 cases of wine per year within five years. Both Craig and I thought that seemed optimistic, but we hoped it would look attractive to a bank.

Every bank in Temecula and Murrieta turned us down. There just wasn't enough collateral in the land, and the idea of us running a winery with zero experience didn't pass the loan committees. Then we approached a bank in Fallbrook, 20 miles south of Temecula. Gerry, Rosie, and Bill met with the president and head loan officer and presented our business plan.

After the loan committee reviewed our files, Bill, Rosie, and Gerry drove to the bank headquarters to hear the verdict. The president began by telling them that based on our family's financials and collateral, the numbers were outside the bank's comfort zone. But, considering the family and its history, they surmised that we'd be a reliable family to entrust with a loan.

Years later, Gerry had lunch with the bank president who had approved our loan. "How the heck did we get approved for a loan back then?" Gerry asked. The president answered, "It was a character loan, in part. There are so many darn Wilsons around, we knew they wouldn't all let it fail."

LEFT PAGE: Bill and Jenifer's humorous Christmas card announcing their move from Mission Viejo. This trailer was used by previous vineyard workers and left on our property. Some of Bill and Jenifer's friends thought this card was serious and that trailer was their new home. RIGHT PAGE: LEFT: Mick and Bill working on the initial winery plans. Christopher and Heather in background. RIGHT: Gerry, Mick, Bill and Craig in our first denim uniform shirts, discussing the winery at the folks' rental home.

This article by Angela Geiser appeared in *The Californian* Newspaper on August 28, 1997:

FAMILY RAISES GRAPES - AND KIDS - AT NEW WINERY

When the Wilsons of Temecula say their new winery will be family-run, they don't mean a couple of family members will be given courtesy titles on the corporate documents. They mean family-run!

Rosemary and Gerald Wilson will serve wine in the tasting room while son, Bill, will manage the winery, daughter, Libby, will coordinate weddings on the site, and son Mick, a pastor, will officiate weddings. Son-in-law, Craig, will sell wine, and daughter-in-law, Jenifer, will help Libby with parties and banquets.

"We're a close family," said Gerald Wilson. "We know sometimes going into business together can break up a family, but we think we can handle the risks."

A contractor has laid the foundation for the 5,400 square-foot winery and tasting room a mile and a half east of the Van Roekel Winery on Rancho California Road. The Wilsons have county approval to construct the Mediterranean-design winery and hope also to gain county go-ahead to operate it as a commercial winery in time to open by spring 1998.

At the same time, the Wilsons build the winery, they are building their knowledge of viticulture—from the ground up. "We don't know what we're doing," admitted Rosemary, but they have made it their mission to learn.

Gerald, a retired vice president of Kemper Financial Services, and Bill have attended half a dozen seminars and wine courses and read every book they could find. They've also asked scores of questions of local winemakers, who shocked the family with their willingness to teach, Bill Wilson said.

If learning about running a winery is challenging, paying for one—without the help of deep corporate pockets—has been daunting.

By the time they open the winery, the Wilsons expect to spend $1 million, some of that for a dozen or so studies or projects that have little to do with the winery itself. A few of the incidentals that must be funded before building a winery included hydrology studies on the creek that runs through the property, biological studies on the endangered gnatcatcher and kangaroo rat, and requirements from the county that they build a left turn lane on Rancho California Road. The Wilsons are seeking outside financing through Fallbrook National Bank and possibly a private investor.

LEFT PAGE: The family inspecting our first wine being made at Thornton Winery. RIGHT PAGE TOP: First section of the steel building. MIDDLE LEFT: Bill and Jenifer (holding Cassidy) with Christopher and a friend on the scissor lift. MIDDLE RIGHT: Christopher and Heather. BOTTOM RIGHT: Cambria's baptism in the lower garden. The steel structure is in the background.

56

THE MAN OF STEEL, OR STEAL

Bill was advised to build the tasting room with a steel frame rather than wood. He liked the idea because it would make the building more fireproof, but it was hard to find an experienced steel contractor. Bill and Gerry finally met one in Northern California who seemed to have the right credentials and reasonable pricing. Gerry and Rosie also found an architect and engineer, all in one person named Oz. To save money, we decided to act as our own general contractor and hire these men as subcontractors.

We eventually got our plans approved by the county, paying the requisite fees at every step. We hired a grader and broke ground. We had to create a large dirt pad, 15 feet above the creek, to protect against the risk of a "100-year flood." We extended the pad to where the rolling vineyards ascended so that vines would surround the winery. When we finished the grading, our family celebrated by sharing a bottle of wine, while sitting in our white, plastic patio chairs.

We had another mini-celebration after we poured the concrete for the footings. But this time, we had our plastic chairs *and* a folding table.

We were excited when we saw giant trucks arriving with our first steel beams for the winery building. We noticed our contractor had decided to buy used steel. But he explained that this was saving us a lot of money and would work fine. He also rented several pieces of construction equipment, including large cranes to hoist the massive beams in place. His team began

cutting and bolting the pieces together. Our building was starting to take shape!

One day we were having a family gathering in the lower garden. The steelwork was underway, and a basic frame had emerged. The mood was positive, with smiles all around. Libby, with a glass of white wine in her hand, stared at the building and commented to Gerry, "Dad, have you taken a look at the tasting room building lately?"

"Yeah, it's coming along, isn't it?" he said with a smile.

Libby replied in a slow and steady voice, "No, it's, um, tilted!"

Bill, overhearing Libby, looked at the building and let out an appropriate "s@#t."

We all turned to look at it. Something was awry. The front half of the building didn't line up with the back half, and the whole thing looked like it was leaning a tad to one side.

Bill immediately reacted, "Yeah, but we can fix that. I'll find out how off it is, and I'll make it right."

But Craig was perturbed. "No, it is really off!" he countered. "This steel contractor has been unprofessional since we hired him. The frame is so askew. I suggest we level the building and start over. It might save us money in the long run. Look, all the major beams are misaligned!"

Early the next day, Bill and the contractor both measured, and, sure enough, the front half was off by two feet. The contractor admitted his mistake. He would have to take down all the beams, recut, and re-weld them. He worked on it for a few weeks until

one day the contractor didn't show up. After repeated efforts to contact him, we concluded he had walked out on us—with no warning or phone call.

We soon found out he had done the same thing to others. But he didn't just leave us with a half-done building. Shortly after he fled, his steel supplier contacted us, asking for payment. It turned out that our contractor hadn't paid for all the steel he obtained. And as the acting general contractor, we were now responsible for it.

Even though we couldn't track down the contractor, we learned that he had recently delivered a whole truckload of the steel we'd purchased to his storage yard an hour north of Temecula. Craig assumed that the contractor's associates would be relocating the steel soon, so he called the steelyard and asked that the supervisor deliver the $65,000 worth of metal to us. However, the supervisor refused to release it. Craig boldly asked again, and the supervisor hung up. Craig found the address on an invoice and drove to the steel yard, unannounced.

Craig arrived at a locked gate and hollered at some workers to let him in, but they ignored him. He then climbed the tall security fence, found the supervisor, confronted him, and demanded that someone drive our steel in their unregistered 18-wheeler to Temecula. The supervisor reluctantly drove it himself and arrived at our property that afternoon. Craig also made calls to get all the rental equipment off our property to stop the daily billing.

Later, the equipment rental company sued us for $60,000 in unpaid rental fees. Our contractor had also stopped paying his workers at the end, so we had to pay them too. And our building was still two feet off. We had a structural and financial mess on our hands. In just one week after we noticed the misaligned steel frame, our dream had become a nightmare.

At this point, naysayers seemed to come out of the woodwork. We began hearing comments like, "I told you so. You all could never make this work!" "This was doomed to fail from the beginning!" The one that got under Bill's skin the most was, "I knew you didn't have what it takes!" But all the derision only strengthened our family's resolve to see it through—especially Bill's.

We approached our dilemma with sarcastic humor. Someone said, "That frame looks like the carcass of a turkey!" It did. And we all felt like one too.

Gerry had maxed out his credit cards on the project, and now he couldn't pay them back. He began getting calls from the creditors. Gerry asked them to be patient and give him some time. The irony of his situation was stark: He had faithfully worked and wisely invested for over 40 years, expecting to retire in security. But now Gerry was dealing with credit card collectors. He laughs about it now, but at the time, it was humbling and painful.

ABOVE: Bill discussing the steel mishap with the contractor in 1997.

THE TAX GEEK

A year before we bought the land, Gerry invested a portion of his retirement money in a high-risk, high-return venture in Arizona on the advice of a financial expert. But there were some fraudulent transactions on the other end and Gerry found out that his investment was lost. Gerry usually is conservative in his finances but this time he had taken a risk with $250,000.

He hired an attorney and went through arbitration. Gerry won the case, but the guy who owed him soon fled, so he only got back $50,000. At least, Gerry thought, he could write off the $200,000 loss on his tax return. But after Gerry filed his return, he was contacted by an IRS worker who demanded complete documentation of the $200,000 loss. Gerry complied, providing every document he could find. But this zealous young IRS officer, whom we named the "Tax Geek," didn't believe Gerry's story. He even called Gerry a liar. Gerry turned to a tax attorney to deal with the IRS.

Rosie was especially incensed by the investment that went bad. "We got fleeced a couple of times," she says, "first by a bad steel contractor, then by a bad investment in Arizona. Then this IRS geek made it even worse."

The case of "Gerry vs. the Tax Geek" went to arbitration, and Gerry eventually won. He could keep the write-off. The Tax Geek was not happy.

We had a construction loan for the tasting room, but Gerry needed funds to get barrels and tanks. He decided to liquidate the IRA he had been building for 25 years. Gerry planned to replenish it within the required 60 days to avoid having the monies taxed. He kept an eye on the calendar.

Two months later, Gerry got a call from his old nemesis, the Tax Geek, informing him that he had taken 61 days to replenish his IRA—one day over the deadline. Bill and Gerry had counted two months, not realizing that one of the months had 31 days. Gerry and Bill drove to the IRS office in Orange County to reason with the Tax Geek and ask for some leniency since Gerry was only one day late.

When the Tax Geek finally came out to meet with Gerry and Bill, he had a sly grin on his face that Gerry described as an "I got you now" smirk. The Tax Geek was so frustrated at losing his previous case with Gerry that he dug into Gerry's records hoping to find something. The one-day delinquency was precisely what the Tax Geek needed to nail Gerry. Gerry's attorney advised him not to fight the IRS as they would likely not budge, and the legal fees would add up quickly. Gerry ended up paying thousands in taxes. What a difference a day makes.

At this time, we needed more money for winemaking equipment and grapes, so Gerry did something humbling—he called his best friend and asked to borrow money. His friend was gracious and generously loaned Gerry $100,000. He asked Gerry not to pay him back monetarily—but in wine. Over the next ten years, we sent him two cases of wine every month. Bill also borrowed money from his good friend, Steve. And Rosie sold some land she owned in Iowa to her family members there. They didn't need to purchase the property but bought it anyway to help her out.

Even with the borrowed money, things were still tough financially. Bill and Gerry would sit in the office trailer

at a long folding table, with all the unpaid bills in three piles. A yellow post-it note marked each stack: NOW, WAIT, IGNORE.

To keep construction costs down, we did as much work as we could ourselves. Bill and I dug trenches and laid all the electrical, phone lines, and water lines. Bill has some carpentry skills, and we had both done a lot of landscaping work at our home in South Pasadena. But in commercial construction, we were completely inexperienced. Many of us wore tool belts for the first time. Gerry jokes that he discovered "self-propelled" screws were not truly self-propelled.

As the work progressed, some family tensions arose. Bill is a *get-'er-done* kind of guy. Craig and I took more of a *let's do it right or don't do it now* approach. Bill was anxious to get the winery open, understandably so. Craig and I didn't want to take risky shortcuts that could hurt us in the long run. A conflict was imminent.

ABOVE: Bill on the scissor lift toasting the start of the steel building with a bottle of our unlabeled Chardonnay with Libby and Craig. Cassidy is with Libby. RIGHT: Cambria helping on the worksite.

THE CONFRONTATION

With all the IRS problems and an AWOL steel contractor, Craig began to see the winery vision slowly collapsing before his eyes. He felt that unless we got better organized, there would never *be* a winery. He perceived that Bill was mismanaging the project and mishandling Gerry's hard-earned retirement money. Something drastic had to happen, or all would be lost.

Craig felt he tried to intervene in small ways to help but was directly or indirectly told by Bill, "Thanks anyway, Craig, but I got it." Bill felt Craig was criticizing from the sidelines at each step, without much skin in the game.

Craig is a New Englander and a diehard Red Sox and Patriots fan. He's also an experienced salesman who has shown great initiative throughout his life. He started a small business and eventually pursued his goal of becoming a golf pro, receiving his PGA card in 1990. His style is direct. But in the Wilson family, we don't like confrontation. We prefer to downplay or ignore relational tension. As Craig simmered, a crisis brewed.

Craig concluded he needed to take a more direct approach with Bill.

One morning in 1998, Craig's patience came to an end. He drove to the winery and found Bill in his office trailer. Bill was fighting walking pneumonia and desper-

ately wanted to be in bed, but he had to deal with the stalled construction and the stacks of bills.

As Craig walked in, he noticed the poster-sized architectural rendering of the finished winery taped to the wall. In stark contrast, the steel frame "turkey carcass" sat just outside the window. Bill was sitting at a table covered with blueprints. Craig approached him calmly.

"Bill," he said, "this is getting nowhere. Libby and I have trusted you to handle this project. But now it's all falling apart. All we have left is that silly steel frame standing out there! Unless something drastically changes, we will all go broke, our families go their separate ways, and the family vision dies."

Bill was thinking; *I don't need this right now. I feel like crap.* Now he was not only sick but experiencing a possible mutiny. He spun in his chair and faced Craig. "Listen, I hear you, but I have been busting my ass here and working eighteen-hour days. So now you decide to jump in the game and start pointing fingers at me?"

Craig didn't back down. "Well, yes! I've tried to help and give suggestions. You always said you 'got it.' But almost every decision has ended in ruin! We need a new direction."

LEFT PAGE: The steel building looking south. RIGHT PAGE: A frustrated Bill remeasuring the building with the steel contractor.

"New direction?" Bill was yelling now. "No, *I* need to make this work. There is no new direction, just the one we are on. *I* can get us back on track."

Craig took a deep breath. "Right now, you are driving this vision into the ground. I think you need to step aside so we can right this ship."

Bill stood up to face Craig. "Step aside? You've got to be kidding! The project is my baby, and I *will* see it through. It *will* be successful. I *will* do whatever it takes."

"Let me clarify," Craig continued. "I am not suggesting that 'you' or 'we' right the ship. I am suggesting that 'I' step in and get this organized. This whole project is sinking, and you are going down with the ship. And you will take Rosie and Gerry with you. I appreciate your hard work thus far, but admit it; the winery is a complete failure."

"A complete failure?" Bill barked. "Really? What are you saying? Are you suggesting I casually walk off the project and let this all collapse?" Bill was now red-faced and yelling even louder.

"Well, no!" Craig snapped back, "We need new leadership. I have a lot of experience organizing things, and I strongly feel I can turn this around."

Bill couldn't believe what he was hearing. Was he being fired? Was Craig taking over? Could he do that? Bill sat back down as he was feeling weak from both his illness and this ambush.

Craig continued, "Libby and I can move into the double-wide, and you and Jenifer can live in town. I can then live close to the project and manage it. Your family can live in a normal house and not have to live like you are camping."

"No frickin' way," Bill shouted. He couldn't believe his ears. "I worked my ass off to get this to this point, and I will finish it. I will not let this fail. I can't let this fail."

Bill took a breath and spoke deliberately, with a tremble in his voice. "I am not an idiot. I am aware of all the mishaps. It grieves me. Listen carefully. I will not step down. I will not leave. Yes, I've made some bonehead decisions, but I've also made some damn good ones. I know all the moving parts, and if I step aside, this is sure to fail. I may have been a major factor in getting us in this mess, but for damn sure, I'm the only one who can get us out of it."

Craig stood his ground, "Bill, I know you have worked hard, and you are all in. Good intentions won't rescue this. New leadership will. I need to take over now. So kindly leave and go get some needed rest."

Bill stood up again slowly, walked within a foot of Craig, and said, "I will not leave. And I will ask this as

nicely as I can—please leave this trailer right now. And I mean now. This conversation is over."

Craig was in a bind. Should he push back and insist Bill leave the construction trailer? Craig might be able to save the project, but would he blow up the family in the process? Or should Craig back down, knowing the project would likely fail under Bill's supervision? Both options seemed like a nightmare.

Craig stood in the office, staring Bill in the eyes. After a few tense seconds, he shook his head in disgust, turned, and quietly left. Stepping out of the trailer, he cursed under his breath.

Inside the trailer, Bill swore out loud.

LEFT PAGE: Bill laying out wire to repair the vine trellises. Gerry is near our Mazda minivan returning from one of his numerous trips to The Home Depot or Hank's Hardware. RIGHT PAGE: Bill expressing frustration while he goes over plans with a subcontractor.

KNEE DEEP IN THE MESS

How did we get into this mess? It depends on whom you ask.

Bill observes, "Gerry doesn't have a mean bone in his body! He always wants to see the good in people. Sometimes they lie to his face, and Gerry tends to believe them. He cares so much about other people. He sees the good in people. Gerry's positivity sometimes gets him into trouble, because some people take advantage of him."

Craig says, "Gerry lost a portion of his hard-earned retirement because of a few unwise investments. I realize Gerry takes 100 percent of the responsibility, but I feel that Bill encouraged Gerry to take those risks. Bill never did a single thing intentionally to hurt anyone or cause problems, but he pulled Gerry into some toxic situations. It seemed like 'hope-and-a-prayer' stuff was just too good to be true."

Libby adds, "Bill was a great picture drawer. He would paint a vision of how great it would be. Yet, Bill truly believed it and felt it in his gut. Bill would present it to Gerry like, 'This will for sure work, I won't let it fail.' But it didn't work."

Libby felt she was the bad guy in all this as she expressed her concern about why Bill and Gerry made some poor decisions together. She asked Dad why he had made such an unwise investment.

Gerry replied, "Bill is doing his best. Maybe stop attacking all the time and try to come alongside Bill."

"Yeah, well, right now, that's hard to do!"

Libby summarizes her perspective: "Bill initiated the winery idea. Bill moved the negotiations along for the first winery we all investigated. Bill researched and landed the acreage we now have. But Bill also got Gerry involved in a risky investment that hurt us. It was Bill, with Gerry's backing, that made it all happen: the good, the bad, and the ugly. We wouldn't be in the family venture without Bill, but we wouldn't be in a financial mess without him as well."

Whoever was to blame, everyone felt the financial pinch. Jenifer describes one particularly low point:

"One crisp morning, as the sun rose over the vineyard, I was in the double-wide looking out the window when I saw a car with two men drive up. We were out in the country, and not many people came to our home, so I was curious. I couldn't believe my eyes as I saw the passenger get out, walk up to our Suburban, open the door, and drive off within one minute! Was it being taken? Who was that guy driving my car? Then it hit me. These men weren't stealing my car—they were repossessing it. They tracked us down and waited until the early morning."

Jenifer called her older brother to ask for a loan so she could get her car back. It was humiliating and depressing for both her and Bill.

Some people gave us well-intentioned advice: "Just cut your losses and sell the used steel." Others said, "Tear down all the steel and rebuild the thing with wood," and "When you are in a hole, stop digging." We all gathered at Rosie and Gerry's house to discuss our options. Should we continue down this road? *Could* we continue?

Bill was the one who consistently said, "Let's do this. Let's go for it. We can make this happen. C'mon!" I wrestled with the increased costs of going forward. Yet, I perceived everyone was financially all-in, and if this winery went south, everyone would be bankrupt. Craig reminded us we still had the option of cutting our losses.

We considered the costs and risks. Gerry reiterated his heart for the family. After some tense discussion, we reached a consensus. We chose to plow ahead. We all felt some reluctance, but we all wanted the family to unite, not blow apart. We kids wanted to see Gerry and Rosie enjoy the last chapters of their life with their family. But to take the next step, we needed to find money to fix our financial mess and hire a new subcontractor to finish the building. We had already tapped our friends and family for loans. Who else could help us out of this financial pit we had dug?

LEFT PAGE: Cambria "helping" plant flowers.

"NEW PLAYERS JOIN WINE COUNTRY"

by J.E. Mitchell. *The Californian, March 9, 1998*

For the Wilson Clan, the sign outside their under-construction winery has been the subject of a running joke.

It seems that the concept of "Coming Soon" has had its meaning redefined—the sign's been there for a while.

But Gerry Wilson says the sign will soon be repainted to say "Open" after construc-tion crews complete the $1.2 million, 8,100 square-foot winery and wine tasting room that is slated to open by this fall.

Wilson, his wife Rosemary, and their son Bill will be the principles in a winery, but the whole family will play a big role in the operation.

"This is about family," said Gerry Wilson, a retired vice president with Kemper Finan-cial Services Inc, as he strolled beneath the metal framework that will soon house the winery's tasting room, deli, and production areas. "That's why we are doing it. I think this takes more guts than brains," Gerry Wilson said. "We're very excited. It's going to be a lot of hard work, but it also looks like a lot of fun."

LOAN #2

Gerry went back to the bank and asked for a second loan on top of the existing construction loan. He hoped that, even with the IRS issues and the bad investments, we might be able to qualify.

One of our bankers, Gary Youmans, believed our dream could get back on track with another loan. He discerned that if the bank didn't lend us more money, our whole family would lose it all. Yet, if we received the loan, he felt our family would bust our tails to make it work. He vouched for us and pushed the loan through all the hurdles at the bank. He qualified us for a Small Business Administration (SBA) loan. We were so thankful he be-lieved in us and worked so hard to help us out. Without that second loan, we would not have made it.

Gerry recalls, "I hear stories about people who have a boatload of money and use it to buy a winery outright. I had just enough to buy the land and get a construction loan to get the project started. Then we had help from friends and another loan from the bank. After that, it was simply a lot of hard work to make it happen."

The new SBA loan was a life preserver. We needed ev-ery dollar—not just to build the winery, but to make the wine!

A REAL STEEL

With the help of the new loan, Bill found a legitimate steel contractor from the San Diego area. These folks were real pros. They commuted 60 miles one way every day to finish the project as quickly as possible. For over three months they cut and welded to resurrect the turkey carcass. They installed the steel studs, put on the roof, and helped with the stucco. Bill was rarely in the office trailer, preferring to work alongside the construction crew and overseeing every step.

We weren't just building a tasting room but a wine production facility too. Even though the building wasn't started, we recognized we needed some wine in time for our planned 1998 grand opening. We had the grapes on our 20 acres, but we didn't yet have our own building to make the wine.

TOP: The building after the good steel company took the project over. LOWER LEFT: Building the deck. LOWER RIGHT: Hayden and Gavin.

WE NEED WINE

There was another small problem—we didn't know how to make wine. Gerry and Rosie had made dandelion and rhubarb wine in their basement in Minnesota, but, as Rosie pointed out, that didn't quite qualify.

Thankfully, we found a local winery that would crush our grapes, then make and bottle the wine for us. We, of course, had to pay them for their services and buy the corks, capsules, bottles, and labels. We also needed to buy more than 20 oak wine barrels at about $450 each. If we didn't, we wouldn't have any red wines for our planned opening in 1998.

Then, to our dismay, we learned we couldn't use our grapes to make wine. Just before we bought the land, the existing vineyard management company had signed a contract agreeing to ship the grapes to Napa Valley for five more years. Even though we were the new owners of the land, the agreement stated we would only be able to get grapes for our wine if there was an excess harvest. We would have to buy our grapes and then have them transported to a local winery to make the wine for us. Bill was furious that this detail had not been clearly communicated. Gerry was frustrated because he had to write a check for his own grapes.

The 1996 harvest was a large one, so we were able to get some Cabernet Sauvignon and Chardonnay grapes in excess of our vineyard manager's contract. We had the grapes picked and sent to Thornton Winery, just four miles down the road. Their winemaker took it from there and produced an amazing 1996 Cabernet Sauvignon and 1996 Chardonnay for us. Our very first red wine sat in barrels at Thornton until late 1997 when they bottled it for us.

FLOWERS FOR WINE

In early 1997, we developed a relationship with a large flower grower in Fallbrook. Bill and I would show up with a few cases of wine, and the grower would let us fill our trailer with slightly old flowers that he couldn't sell to The Home Depot or Lowe's. For the first five years of the winery, we planted every flower bed with these hand-me-down flowers that we nursed back to life. Rosie was the one who trimmed and resurrected each of them. I estimated that we planted over 4,000 flowers during those first five years.

We hoped to do the same in 1997 with some excess Cabernet and Chardonnay. The Chardonnay grapes were picked in August and processed at another winery. A few weeks later, the vineyard manager's crew then harvested more than ten tons of beautiful Cabernet grapes and placed them in 20 half-ton bins. The crew left at dawn, assuming the grapes would be picked up by the local winery for processing.

Those grapes sat all morning in the hot August sun. Bill called the winery and asked why they hadn't picked up the grapes. The trucks finally arrived around noon and their crew loaded them up.

That afternoon, Bill got a call from the winery. They received the grapes but couldn't process them because there was too much spoilage. Every half-ton bin was affected, and the winemaker had to dump them all. No one would claim responsibility, and we didn't have any signed contracts, so we ended up with no 1997 Cabernet Sauvignon, even though we'd paid $8,000 for 25 bins of grapes. However, our 1997 Chardonnay was fine.

LEFT PAGE: Local Winemakers, MarshalL Stuart and John MacPherson helping Craig, Libby, and Rosie check out our wine at Callaway. RIGHT PAGE: Rosie in the lower garden planting some flowers we traded for wine. Taffy and Merlot helping with harvest.

FIRED UP

One Spring weekend, Bill and I grabbed chain-saws and cleared out more dried branches and sticks from the creek bed. We piled them on a large, flat dirt area between the lower garden and the main road. The ten-foot pile got too huge to haul to the dump, so we decided to torch it. We planned to burn one part of the pile at a time so that we wouldn't attract attention. We knew that to do it right, we'd need a burn permit from the county. But we figured if we just burned a section at a time we'd be okay.

We waited until dark and lit the branches. To our surprise, the entire pile quickly caught fire and burned gloriously. The flames rose 30 feet into the night sky. There was nothing flammable nearby to catch, so we didn't fear the fire spreading. We had a small garden hose in case the fire spread outside the large pile. As we stared in awe at the flames, a fire engine came screeching around the corner, lights flashing and sirens blazing. Rosie was standing near the burning pile with the weakly-flowing garden hose in her hand, which did not affect the fire at all.

As the engine captain approached, Rosie looked up from her job on the garden hose and said to him, "Wow, look how many firefighters are here! But we've got this under control. Thanks anyway for checking!" She smiled and turned back to her garden hose.

The captain didn't smile but nodded at one of his crew members who pulled out a huge firehose and doused the fire in 20 seconds. "Mrs. Wilson," the captain said, "we love the work you're doing on this property, but please get a burn permit next time." Rosie agreed, and as the engine crew drove off, she turned her small garden hose back to the soaked, smoldering wood to make sure it was all out.

WORKING HALF-TIME

1998-2000

Our construction losses and "Coming Soon" sign were becoming big news in the Temecula Valley. Here's an excerpt from the April 28, 1998 edition of *The Californian:*

> Ultimately, the family found itself owing thousands of dollars. Last year's El Niño weather also threw work behind schedule.
>
> "I had to sell my house in Orange County, but the wine is good," Bill Wilson said.
>
> About 3,000 cases of Wilson Creek wine are stored over at Thornton Winery he said, which is mostly Chardonnay and Cabernet, with a small amount of bottles of a Rhone blend.
>
> Bill Wilson said he's pleased with the work being done now by the construction team, even though the family has had to scale back some of its elaborate plans to save money. That means leaving out the Italian marble and other flourishes now and adding them in later.
>
> "We're doing what it takes to get open," he said.
>
> Once the winery is open, the Wilsons will be able to sell the wine on their own premises, as well as offer tastings and make wine by themselves.
>
> "We hope to one day be able to use all of our own grapes, and not sell them," Bill Wilson said. "But our goal is to stay small and family-owned. We don't want to be a mega-winery."

We all continued to work on the landscaping and construction together. As Bill quips, "We work half-days; which twelve hours you choose is up to you." Fortunately, Bill is very good at recruiting people and pulling them alongside. With his relational skills, he was able to get a lot of people to partner with us. Meanwhile, Gerry was making constant trips to supply stores to keep the crews working.

LEFT: The pile of branches growing higher in lower right corner of the photo. RIGHT: Craig and Libby with friend Mike Formella, at the Balloon & Wine Festival. RIGHT PAGE: Mick & Bill building the wood chip walkway in the lower garden area.

WINE AND SOFTBALL - 1997-2000

Craig and Libby wanted to meet people and advertise our soon-to-be family winery, so they started a Wilson Creek co-ed softball team. They recruited people from their childbirth classes and neighbors from across the street. Rosie was the scorekeeper. The team's jerseys had "Wilson Creek" emblazoned on the front and "Win or Lose, we always booze" printed on the sleeves. The team enjoyed wine and beer after each game and eventually won a league championship.

The softball team helped us pour wine at key events. The first was The Temecula Valley Balloon and Wine Festival in 1998. We poured unlabeled bottles, as our new labels hadn't been printed yet. Libby hand-wrote the name of the wine on each bottle with a gold pen. She recalls what it was like being the newcomers at the festival amidst more established wineries:

"We begged people to taste our wine. Next to us was the established Thornton Winery. They had a significant following, with what seemed like 20 people in line during the whole festival. They had fancy grape design tablecloths and very elegant wine buckets that set them apart as a classy winery. They also had good wine! And there we were with handwritten bottles. Funny thing is that we had a wine that they had made for us. Over time we enticed people to come over to taste ours as well."

The softball team also volunteered at a 1999 Taste of Temecula event where guests would visit multiple wineries over a weekend. We were allowed to participate even though we weren't officially open yet. Each winery paired their wines with a particular food. Rosie wanted to make her popular Chinese chicken salad and pair it with our recently bottled Chardonnay.

The local restaurant, Prestos, made summer squash soup. We served the soup out of a large kettle the size of a trash can. Rosie made her salad and put it in a large camping cooler. Gerry hand-shredded all the chicken the previous night and Rosie prepared the salad from crates of lettuce. The softball team served the food and poured our wines, and we paid them in wine and lunch. Rosie's Chinese chicken salad was a big hit. In the end, she bagged up extra salads for every volunteer to take home.

The team also liked trading their labor for wine. When the printer finally delivered our labels, we learned that their unique shape made it impossible for Thornton Winery's bottling machine to apply them, so we had to put them all on by hand. At that time we had over 300 cases of Chardonnay and 400 cases of Cabernet, with twelve bottles in each case. We needed help. So after the Friday night games, Craig gathered the team in our unfinished warehouse to help. He developed an assembly line with rows of chairs and rectangular folding tables. Craig ordered pizza and iced the beer. Of course, they would also open some bottles of our unlabeled wine. We noticed that, at first, our inexperienced volunteers often applied the labels crooked. Then as they got the hang of it, the labels got straighter. Then as the evening progressed and the volunteers consumed more wine, the labels got crooked again.

Whole families would come and enjoy the fun, energetic vibe. The kids used the huge warehouse as their personal playground, riding their tricycles and Big Wheels on the outside walkways. We paid only in wine, but those were some of the best times in our startup years. The team boasted that they "worked for wine."

OUR FIRST SALE

One day the softball team and family were pouring our wine at our second Temecula Balloon and Wine Festival. Bill and Jenifer were there enjoying the experience. She recalls: "We had such a good product and others were enthused and excited for us. People loved the family vibe and the wine. This festival gave us an upswing. We thought to ourselves, *Hey, maybe we do have something here! Maybe we did something right in working with the local winery in the making of our wines because people love our Chardonnay and Cabernet!*"

Around 5:00 p.m., a female festival employee came to our booth and said to Bill, "You can't pour wine now! It's against the ABC, and you'll get us all in trouble!" She was referring to the Department of Alcoholic Beverage Control, and the strict festival rule that the pouring of alcohol must stop at 5:00. "You've gotta stop!" the employee railed, "And I mean now!" Bill told her we would comply, and we did shut down on time. After a few minutes, a vendor from a few booths down approached Bill. "My wife brought me a taste of your Chardonnay, and it is one of the best Chardonnays I have ever had. Can I buy a bottle?"

"Sorry, I just can't do it," Bill said reluctantly. "Our winery isn't open yet, and this wine isn't legally labeled. Plus, we had to shut down at 5:00."

"Aw, come on, man! How much do you want for the bottle?"

The man was flashing some actual greenbacks, which Bill hadn't seen in a long time.

"I can't do it, as much as I would like to! ABC people are floating all around here."

"In that case," the vendor exclaimed, "I am going to steal a bottle!"

Bill chuckled and calmly said, "Sorry, the wine needs to stay here. I gotta walk away and pack up our wine. Have a good evening."

As Bill turned away, he glanced back and witnessed the "customer" quickly reach down into the cooler, grab a bottle, drop it down the front of his pants, then flee around the corner.

Bill said, "Wow! That was the first bottle of wine we've ever had stolen!" He was impressed that somebody loved our wine so much that he'd be gutsy enough to steal it—right in front of him. *God bless him for it!* Bill thought.

A few minutes later, as Rosie emptied the ice from the large cooler, she noticed a bill floating in the water. She reached in, held up a dripping-wet 20-dollar bill, and exclaimed, "Who put this money in the cooler, for heaven's sake?"

Bill laughed and exclaimed, "That stolen bottle is our first sale, ever!"

> "That stolen bottle is our first sale, ever!"

LEFT PAGE: Softball team getting pizza after a game. RIGHT PAGE: TOP: Libby and Jenifer at Temecula Valley Balloon & Wine Festival. BOTTOM: Gerry in the white baseball hat at the same festival.

"We had the dream, we had the faith, and, more importantly, we had the support of the community because people met us as we worked on the winery and as we slowly became involved in the community."

THE PROJECT THAT CREATED A COMMUNITY

There's an old Scandinavian folk story in which a hungry traveler comes to a village carrying nothing but a large cooking pot. He approaches several villagers and asks them for some food, but they all turn him away. So, he walks into the middle of town, puts his big pot down, fills it with water, and drops a large stone into it. Then he starts a fire under it as the villagers begin to gather around.

"What is that?" one of them asks.

The stranger responds, "I'm making stone soup. It tastes wonderful. And I'd love to share some with you! But I think it needs some seasoning."

"Oh, I have some," a villager says. "I'll go and get it." He returns with some spices and throws them into the pot. Another villager says, "I think you need at least some carrots."

"Yes! Can you go find some?"

The villager brings some carrots and tosses them into the pot.

Someone else asks, "What's that? Carrot soup? Well, we need some onions and chicken!"

One by one, the villagers bring what they think the soup needs and toss it into the pot. Soon, they've made an enormous pot of tasty soup. The entire village has a big party at the end of the day, enjoying the soup they've made together.

After the celebration, the stranger quietly takes the empty pot to the next village.

That parable is a good description of Wilson Creek Winery in the early days. From around 1996 to 1999, our family was the stranger, and the winery was the empty pot. Over time, people seemed to appreciate our family hospitality and vision. They began to come and help, contributing however they could. We built an extended family of friends, neighbors, construction workers, government administrators, local winery staff, suppliers, and anyone else who shared our vision for family. We exchanged wine for labor.

We even traded a wedding for labor as a local firefighter named Larry helped us install pipe during his off-hours. Larry also helped pour a concrete walkway to our newly-built wedding gazebo—because he was having his wedding there the next day!

A friendly neighbor helped us with construction framing and drywall. Another friend helped with electrical projects. A local agricultural business coached me in how to control plant pests, what grows where, and when to water and fertilize. A retired deputy sheriff helped install floorboards in the tasting room. A local golf pro helped us with painting. Our cousin, Doug, used his eighteen-wheeled flatbed truck to drop off free loads of used railroad ties. These helpers would leave with some wine and, often, some leftovers from Rosie. And they always left with a smile.

Why did so many people help our family? I think when they discovered we weren't in Temecula to be *takers*, people gravitated toward that and wanted to help us. Givers attract givers. Our extended family truly helped get us off the ground and spread the news about this new family winery. As Bill puts it, "We had the dream, we had the faith, and, more importantly, we had the support of the community because people met us as we worked on the winery and as we slowly became involved in the community."

We did all the landscaping ourselves. And even though we weren't open, we held some private weddings in our lower garden area. Jenifer and Rosie could often be found in the front, planting flowers past midnight in preparation for a wedding the next day.

LEFT PAGE: Bill working on the sidewalk and patio to the gazebo. RIGHT PAGE: LEFT TO RIGHT: Jenifer's brother Michael, volunteering with crush. Rosie planting flowers with Cambria and friend. Don Galleano at Galleano Winery just south of Rancho Cucamonga with Deanna and Sarah on bottom. Staff members Sheila and Chris are with Rosie and Gerry.

TRIPLE-WIDE GOOD NEWS FOR THE FOLKS - 1998

It was evident to Rosie and Gerry there wouldn't be enough funds to build their two-story Italian villa dream home on the hill. But Rosie found another option when she visited a friend's newly-purchased manufactured home. Rosie loved the vaulted ceilings and numerous windows and realized it would be a perfect fit.

I wanted to help my parents make an informed decision, knowing that this might be the home where they'd live out the later chapters of their lives. So, I went with them to a manufactured home dealer and helped negotiate a fair price. Three months later, their newly-completed home arrived in three parts pulled by three semi-truck cabs. The dirt pad had already been permitted and graded with the help of a local friend who had a tractor. The sections were carefully brought together and placed on piers. Bill and I helped to install the septic and water. We also dug trenches from the winery to the home to tap into the winery's electrical and water. A year later, we put a block foundation under it and erected a garage. Their house still stands on the hill today, and Rosie and Gerry cannot imagine living anywhere else. "We love overlooking the winery," Rosie says. "There is a beautiful view of vines from every window, as our home is in the midst of the Chardonnay vineyard. It is magical! We wake up to hot air balloons, and at night I feel like I could practically touch the stars. We walk a hundred feet to the winery, with a cup of coffee in our hands. The dogs just love it too. We feel like this is heaven on earth."

OLD 84 SINGLE-WIDE

While the family worked on the landscaping and winery construction from 1996-1999, I lived in the Pasadena area and drove to Temecula as often as possible to help. I then worked in a church in the Sacramento area. While there, I met Deanna at a church where I was preaching. We became friends and eventually started dating.

After a year up north, I knew I wanted to be back in the family business, so I moved to Temecula. At 33 years old, I was frustrated that I had no career and I was sleeping in my parents' guest room and then on the floor of the wedding trailer. But I was glad to be part of the family venture full-time. Eventually, I bought a used single-wide mobile home for $3,500 and had it transported to the property. When it arrived, I barely recognized it. The movers had hastily shoved the slideouts into the main home and boarded up every door and window. It looked like a beat-up shoebox with plywood sheets slapped all over it. I knew we had some work to do to resurrect this monstrosity. The address nailed to it was #84, so we called it "Old 84."

Bill and the winery crew helped me fix it up. It required a lot of work, but that old single-wide found a special place in my heart. Living there, I finally felt fully committed to my family and the business. When Deanna and I were married, "Old 84" was the first place we lived as a couple.

Mobile homes were becoming a conspicuous presence on the property. Deanna and I were in the single-wide, Bill and Jenifer in a double-wide, and Gerry and Rosie in their triple-wide. We began referring to ourselves, jokingly, as "trailer trash." But I loved living in the trailer. They were a gift to us, enabling us to live in the vineyards close to each other.

LEFT PAGE: TOP TO BOTTOM: Bill and Jenifer's double-wide. MIDDLE: One third of the folks' home being delivered. BOTTOM: Mick and Deanna at Old 84 with Merlot and Max. RIGHT PAGE: Christopher driving the tractor during harvest.

BEGINNING UPS AND DOWNS

Christopher, Cassidy, Cambria and friends hanging out on the trampoline we erected next to the incompleted tasting room. The new triple-wide manufactured home can be seen on the hill. We kept the trampoline up for the kids until we had an outside barrel tasting event in which we discovered four intoxicated guests bouncing on the trampoline. The trampoline was promptly relocated up the hill near Bill's double-wide so we wouldn't have any guest accidents.

PB&J TIME - 1999

Since we weren't open yet, we still had a ton of expenses but no income. As usual, we had to make every penny count. If there was one person who could do that, it was Rosie. She had always been frugal, shopping at discount stores and thrift stores, as she still does today. So, during this financial pinch, Rosie did what she does so well—she tightened the straps and made it work.

Rosie bought bread, peanut butter, and jelly at the 99 Cents Only store, then made us sandwiches and had a gallon of milk handy to wash it all down. She once tried making powdered milk and pouring it into an empty gallon milk container, but that didn't fool anybody. We all laughed at her valiant attempt to save money, but it was gross. As Rosie jokes today, "We had peanut butter sandwiches day after day for lunch; then, for dinner, we'd binge by having peanut butter *and* jelly, with our wine, of course." That phase took a toll on Rosie, as she recounts: "I have not eaten a peanut butter sandwich since we opened our doors in 2000! I bait the mouse traps with peanut butter. But I can't eat it anymore. Peanut butter cookies are alright, but not a PB&J—*ever* again!"

OPERATION WE "WERE NEVER OPEN" - JANUARY 2000

We created a landscaped property with flowers, walkways, and a large gazebo. We also had good wine. We felt we would be successful, but we just had to get open. The exterior of the building looked finished, so people driving by often pulled in and asked for a wine tasting. Limos and shuttles came in with their guests. As much as we wanted to accommodate them, we weren't officially open and couldn't say we were. We grew tired of turning people away.

In 1999 we participated again in the Temecula Valley Barrel Tasting. We couldn't sell bottles of wine, but we could let people taste our reds. Numerous people liked our wine and then asked to buy some of our 1996-1998 bottled wines. Thanks to the softball team, the bottles were now labeled, but because we were not officially open, we still couldn't sell any. We also weren't supposed to have people in the tasting room, so we held the event outside. But as more people came, Bill suggested we at least open the tasting room for a few hours, which we did.

Then Bill suggested we sell a few bottles to those who asked—just for this weekend. We all rationalized the decision since, after all, we were almost open. That was our first time entertaining the public in our tasting room. And for the first time, we sold some wine; Gerry even signed some bottles. One of the singers from the rhythm and blues group *The Drifters* happened to be there. In a magical moment, he ended up singing "Under the Boardwalk" a capella for an impromptu audience in our sparse tasting room. The acoustics were incredible, and about 30 people at the bar all sang along.

That moment gave us some needed encouragement: maybe we could get this winery open and get through these dark times. We adapted the line from the movie *Field of Dreams,* saying it to ourselves, "If you build it, they will come!"

Every county department signed off on the winery, except one. Once the county health department completed their inspection, we'd be able to get our occupancy permit. We anticipated it would happen in December '99.

LEFT PAGE: TOP: Bill behind the bar with Rosie. BOTTOM: Gerry and Mick serving on the tasting room patio soon after we opened. ABOVE: Cambria and Cassidy playing in a sparse tasting room.

We planned a Y2K grand opening on New Year's Eve, but that date came and went. We threw a New Year's party anyway in the warehouse with over 150 friends and family.

In the first few weeks of January, people drove in repeatedly and asked, "Are you open?" We had made an exception for the barrel tasting event. But should we now start selling wine—without a permit? The temptation was strong. We had the proper licenses from the state and federal governments; we just needed the county's approval. So, as more and more people approached us, we wrestled with the decision. Bill said, "We have to sell wine to pay that pile of bills. Let's go ahead and sell some more bottles. We have done everything right; we're just waiting on the county health department."

I was okay with a little risk, but selling wine without a permit made me nervous. "Yes, we need the money," I said. "But we should probably hold off until we get final approval."

"I say we sell it," Bill responded.

I cringed. "Do you want to go to jail—or see Gerry go to jail?"

"No one is getting arrested. We have the approval to sell wine. We are waiting on approval to sell wine *here*. We have approvals from nine out of ten county departments. Isn't 90 percent an A grade?"

I could see I was losing the battle. I envisioned a mug-shot of Gerry on the front page of the local newspaper with the caption: *Local Father and Winery Owner Jailed.*

"Okay, if we do it, then let's make sure we can quickly make the tasting room look as though we never sold wine here when the inspector comes."

The next day, we started to welcome curious guests and sell some bottles. To attract more people, we parked our cars in the lot to make it look as though we had numerous customers. Our inspection was coming in a few weeks, so we prepared our plan: "Operation *We Were Never Open.*" Bill gave direction, "When the inspector comes, flip the tasting room to make it look like we hadn't ever served or sold wine. Clear any evidence of wine sales. Move anything that might look suspicious, such as wine glasses, open wine bottles, wine price signs, and the small cash register, and relocate it to Rosie and Gerry's house. Also, remove from the kitchen any indication that Rosie was cooking lunches for the staff."

The day before the official inspection, the entire family flew into action. Jenifer moved the cash register, Libby and Craig helped to remove the bottles, Bill removed wine sales signs, and I made sure every bit of evidence was out of sight. We did a pretty good job, as the tasting room now looked sparse. I even put the large sign back up at the entrance that read *Opening Soon, Under Construction.*

The inspector drove up at the appointed time, with a clipboard and an expression that said *I mean business.* He scrutinized every little thing while Bill followed close behind to answer any questions. After a thorough going-over, the inspector walked toward the cashier area near the front entrance. Our whole family gathered discreetly within earshot to listen. Without changing his facial expression, the inspector approached Gerry. "I have to congratulate you on your wines. You have nice reds here."

Gerry looked nervous. "Uh, th-thank you."

"Well, yes! I was here a couple of weeks ago tasting wine. It was great! I bought a bottle of your Cabernet Sauvignon. You even signed a bottle for me."

Gerry winced, "We're busted, aren't we?"

The inspector then took a pen out of his shirt pocket and began filling out a document in triplicate.

I thought, *Oh, crap, here comes the citation. Will there be handcuffs?*

We waited as he wrote.

The inspector signed the document, then tore off the yellow copy and handed it to Gerry. "You can all relax. I didn't find any problems. You passed. Congratulations! Here is your Certificate of Occupancy. You are now officially open!"

We were stunned. We looked at each other and realized we weren't going to jail! We hugged and high-fived each other, trying not to be too happy in front of the inspector. Gerry shook his hand and thanked him profusely. Bill gave him a bear hug. When the inspector finally walked out of the tasting room, we all burst into cheers. Gerry's eyes welled up with joy. After all our obstacles, mishaps, and hard work, we had done it. We were finally open for business.

Sarah with her dad, Mick.

DISCOVERING BUBBLES - DECEMBER 1999

Bill's wife, Jenifer, wanted Champagne for the Y2K Millennium Celebration we were planning at the winery. She was also looking for a good Champagne to serve at the weddings we were now doing. Bill knew Jenifer wanted something unique, so he contacted a Champagne producer in Northern California and asked them to ship us some samples. Bill and Jenifer chose the Brut and a slightly sweeter Champagne. The producers shipped down ten cases for the New Year's party. Over 150 people attended.

A few days after the party, Bill called the producer and asked, "We liked what you sent, but do you have anything else interesting we can try—something different that no one else has?"

They said, "We're working on a blend. We kind of like it, but it is in its experimental phase."

"What is it?"

"It is almond-flavored Champagne."

"What? Almond-flavored? I never heard of that, but for the heck of it, can you ship us some cases when its ready?"

A few months later the ten cases arrived on a Friday at 3:00 p.m. We served it to staff and curious guests. By noon the next day, all ten cases were consumed or sold. We looked at each other and said, "Wow! What just happened? What is it about this stuff?"

Bill ordered 55 more cases. They lasted a week. Then he ordered 55 more and they went quickly as well. We began working with the producer to come up with our own recipe and label.

We all liked the Almond Champagne but thought it was too sweet. Over the next month, Bill worked with the sparkling wine producer to come up with a variation that was slightly sweet but had some nice mouth-watering acidity to it. He drove up to nail down the sweetness level with the producer and brought back some samples of the new formula. We all loved it.

When the producer bottled and shipped a few pallets of our recipe down, the staff and customers went even crazier. A few months after we opened, a guest who had tasted the Almond bought 50 cases and had us ship them to Florida for his wedding.

Almond Champagne fit our demographic—it was fun, slightly sweet, and different. And it brought in revenue to help us take the next step. As Rosie says, "It was the Almond that put us on the map."

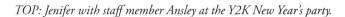

TOP: Jenifer with staff member Ansley at the Y2K New Year's party.

85

FIRST WEDDING

We were excited to host our first paid wedding in May of 2000. The soon-to-be bride looked over our grounds and liked what she saw, even though we hadn't completed the gazebo or the landscaping. She booked her wedding date, trusting it would all be ready in time.

We had more than a dozen projects to complete before the big day; there was dirt where there should have been grass and construction equipment lying all around. But we scrambled. We installed a sprinkler system to get ready for the sod we'd need to plant. We planted as many flowers as we could, while Bill and our construction crew worked late hours to finish the warehouse and parking lot.

On a cold, rainy afternoon four days before the wedding, Jenifer was in her double-wide when she heard a loud knock on the door. Standing on the doorstep was the bride, soaking wet and frustrated. "Look at this place," she said. "It is a mud pit. Will you have this ready before my ceremony?"

Jenifer reassured her we would, but privately wondered whether it would be possible.

Over the next few days, the rain subsided. We put up split rail fencing and planted hundreds of flowers. A few days before the wedding Bill told the groom, "We have time to put in sod or paint the gazebo, but not both." The groom chose the grass. So one day before the wedding we poured the concrete walkways and installed over 2,000 square feet of sod. Fortunately, the bride liked the raw, rustic look of the rough-sawn lumber. After that wedding, we painted the gazebo white.

Bill summarizes our long journey:

"Yeah, we made a lot of mistakes, but we did a lot of things well. The right heart, in the long run, worked out. There were times where we almost didn't make it until a last-minute cash flow would come through. It was a nail-biting time! It was messier than expected, but that's okay. Handling the challenges and crises is better than the sterile idea of reading books on how to start a business, then do steps one, two, three, and four. There was disorder many times. I thought we had it all laid out. Then we jumped into it, and all of a sudden, chaos erupted. Then we somehow made it all work and kept moving forward."

Gerry expressed his perspective when a reporter came to interview him the next day. "In the 1980s, I visited Temecula for business and golf at Temecula Creek Inn," Gerry said. "If someone then told me I would soon be living in Temecula, I would have thought they were crazy. If they then told me that we would eventually own a winery there, I would tell them they were certifiably insane."

We knew we had something special, so starting in early 2000, each family member went out and poured free samples of Almond Champagne at as many charitable events as possible. The word spread.

Bill says, "As good as our red and white wines are, the Almond is in a completely different category. When people visit the winery, they come to find a unique experience, and when they find something different, they tell their friends. That has been a key to our success."

People either love Almond Champagne, or they think it's too sweet. One day an impeccably-dressed couple drove up in a red Ferrari convertible. The husband went to the restroom while the wife came to the tasting bar. I poured her a taste of Almond Champagne. She sipped it, paused, then quietly said, "My husband buys me Cristal, Dom Perignon—anything I want. But how do I tell him that I prefer, uh, *this?*" An hour later I saw one of our wine servers helping the man cram six cases of Almond Champagne into the trunk of that little sports car.

Rosie says, "Coca Cola has their recipe, Pepsi has theirs, and we have ours. We created a winning recipe, then marketed the heck out of it. We went through a lot of effort to pour it at all kinds of events, because if you only look at it and haven't tried it, you may pass it up. Early on, we'd say, 'Try this,' and customers would say, 'Well, I don't like Champagne.' We would get them to taste it, and a typical response was, 'Oh my gosh!' So, our trademark is 'The *Oh my gosh!* Champagne.'"

We ordered refrigerator magnets in the shape of small, yellow yield signs that read, "Zero to naked in 1.2 bottles of Almond Champagne." We then put the saying on T-shirts and large metal, yellow warning signs. I wrote the description on the tasting notes: "This Almond Champagne pairs well with hot tubs, brunches, picnics, and fireplaces." We set out to put a little fun in wine, and people identified with that.

The Almond Champagne was the right wine at the right time. I truly feel that it was a gift from above. After all the grief we had endured getting our winery open, it was as if God was encouraging us: *I know what you went through as a family. So, here is a little present to help you get back on your feet. Enjoy.*

It all started with Almond Champagne. We now have ten flavors!

GRAND OPENING PARTY

The Certificate of Occupancy allowed us to open our doors to the public in April 2000. The local newspaper, *Valley News,* took note: "With no background in vineyard management or winemaking, it was a tough go, but in less than four years, the Wilson family opened the winery for business."

Bill reflects, "How did we get open? We were too stupid to know any better, but smart enough to make it work. It still baffles my whole being. I am so proud of what we accomplished. We're the average American family. We just figured that if we were passionate and loved what we are doing, others who visited would love it too. Had we known how difficult and stressful it would be on the family, we probably wouldn't have done it. Well, actu-ally, we would have because going through all that made us who we are today."

The tasting room quickly became a busy place. When Bill and Gerry wrote our business plan for the construc-tion loan, they estimated we would have 250 visitors a week. That's why we built a relatively small tasting bar—20 feet long—and designed a small production facility behind the tasting room. We also constructed two small restrooms, with one toilet in the ladies' room and a toilet and urinal in the men's room. We built a small office with two desks and a nine-by-nine room for the future wine lab. Our parking lot had 30 approved parking spaces. Surely that would be sufficient.

But we were amazed as more people kept coming.

October 2002

Within a few months, we were welcoming about 500 guests a week. We knew we needed to make our opening public, so we planned an official grand opening. For the Wilsons, that meant throwing a big party and inviting everyone we knew. Craig organized most everything—the invitations, event permits, tickets, live music, food, staff, volunteers, publicity, and Porta-Potties.

We chose Saturday, October 14, as that was Rosie's birthday. We invited friends, family, local business owners, all our construction workers (except the contractor who stiffed us, and eventually ended up in jail), government officials, and staff from the other 14 wineries. We estimated about 400 guests. Instead, over 1,400 showed up.

That grand opening brought back sweet memories of the parties we'd once held in South Pasadena. I recognized several familiar themes: More guests showed up than we expected; we warmly greeted each person; guests had a fantastic time; cars were parked two blocks down the street; and there was a tangible family vibe that drew in people. We had clowns and face painting for the kids, and grape stomping for the adults. Toward the end, everyone sang "Happy Birthday" to Rosie. Unlike those parties though, the police didn't try to shut us down. In fact, some local law enforcement donated their time to help us with security at the grand opening.

We didn't know it then but our greatest adventures were yet to come.

PART THREE: MAKING IT WORK

"If the Wilson family moved to Texas or Timbuktu, it'd be the same thing. It wouldn't be a strategy; it would be who we are; we would start loving people. With the winery, all of a sudden the business is the vehicle for that love. I think that's what has helped Wilson Creek succeed— people picked up on that vibe."

- Bill

2000-2002

EVERYONE DOING EVERYTHING

We were open. Now we needed to figure out how to run a winery. Each family member had some experience in business or hospitality, but running a winery was a different animal. We figured, since we got this open, maybe we could make it work? The whole family jumped in and did whatever was needed.

Gerry greeted the guests and continued to make supply runs. He and Jenifer scrubbed the toilets. Rosie maintained the rose bushes and gardens while greeting guests and conducting tours. Libby ran human resources and helped with weddings—all while continuing her job as a flight attendant. Craig helped with the warehouse construction. I eased into marketing part-time, and oversaw the design and production of wine labels. I helped with the construction and landscaping, and mowed the lawn weekly. Deanna, who moved to Temecula in 2002, helped launch the distribution of our wines to local stores and restaurants. Jenifer handled the purchasing for our gift shop and worked as a cashier. She also made bank deposits, sold weddings, and scrubbed restroom grout. Bill, as usual, did a little bit of everything: overseeing the winemaking and new construction, greeting guests, conducting tours, and helping with shipping. And, as the need arose, we all pitched in to serve wine to more and more guests.

Our four golden retrievers had the job of greeting everybody with big smiles and wagging tails. Meanwhile, Bill and Jenifer's girls—ages two and four—spent hours riding their tricycles around the walkways. As Gerry jokes, "If we didn't have dogs and grand-kids around, I would hire them just to be around—because that is who we are."

From the beginning, Rosie took on the task of making lunch every day for the family and volunteers. That continued even as we grew and hired more staff. They could all stay on the grounds and eat a home-cooked meal every day instead of driving into town. Rosie used those lunchtimes to get to know our volunteers and staff. She liked to know everything about everyone.

TOP: Rosie and Gerry in the tasting room. MIDDLE: Libby, Rosie and Deanna helping Bill blend wines. BOTTOM: Sarah helping to keep things clean. RIGHT PAGE: TOP: Cassidy and Cambria helping Bill and Jenifer label wine with a new machine we bought.

Jenifer reflects on those early times:

"We were shaking up wine country a bit. We were hands-on. We were making it happen because it was our baby. If we didn't put in one hundred fifty percent, it wouldn't work. People saw us digging, building, scrubbing, gardening, painting, and mowing. Every Wilson helped pour the wine. Guests loved seeing family members around. We were all-in, and people wanted to be a part of it. Our reputation grew in the valley as a place that was down-to-earth and run by a hardworking family. The community respected the family, and they loved the dogs! The first question many people ask when they visit the winery is, 'Where are your dogs?' Wilson Creek is truly a family-owned-and-operated winery."

"Welcome to the world of being a winemaker."

MAKING OUR OWN WINE

Bill designed the winery with an attached warehouse that would hold numerous tanks, barrels, and a bottling line. We had to get some initial equipment, so we purchased some used oak barrels and financed four fermentation tanks. We also bought a winepress, a de-stemmer, and some other crushing equipment. But we needed a winemaker. Some local winemaking consultants were willing to help us initially, but we knew we needed someone dedicated to Wilson Creek.

Mike Calabro was a promising winemaker who had already won some amateur awards. He was also a building contractor who was between projects. He wanted to see a grape harvest firsthand, so offered to come help us with construction—and he'd be willing to work for wine. At the time, our consulting winemaker was too busy to help us onsite; he could only give us advice over the phone. We were desperate for in-person help.

When Bill asked Mike to come and help us, the budding winemaker broke into a huge grin. "Well," he said, "it sounds like the same thing that I do with five

gallons, I simply do with 2,000 gallons." Neither Mike nor Bill had expected that Mike would be our winemaker. But he began working for us part-time and within a year he was on board full-time.

Mikey, as he is known, learned the world of large production winemaking the hard way—on the job. One month into his full-time role, Mikey was pumping wine from one tank into another using a large, two-inch-wide hose. He didn't securely connect the end and wine shot out like a full-pressured fire hose spraying red juice all over the tanks, floor, and Bill. Mikey quickly shut the pump off, turned to a wine-soaked Bill and said, "I think I just lost my amateur status."

Bill responded, "Welcome to the world of being a winemaker."

MORE COMPLEXITY, MORE STAFF

We still thought our winery would be a relatively small operation, so the remarkable growth caught us by surprise. As Bill recalls, "We hoped for 5,000 cases in five years but did 15,000 cases in year two. That's the good news. The bad news is that we did 15,000 cases in year two in a winery designed to do 5,000 cases." The facility was being stretched, along with the family.

We increasingly had to deal with complex business issues, such as working with the Alcoholic Beverage Control, the Trade and Tax Bureau, local governments, corporate taxes with the IRS, employee and property insurance, etc. We quickly outgrew what we knew. We needed to bring in people with more experience. So, we moved on from our "yellow pad and cigar box" accounting and hired a professional bookkeeper.

In 2000, we had about twelve paid staff and numerous volunteers. By 2002 our staff numbered over 50, so we hired a full-time human resources manager. We also hired our own vineyard manager, tasting room manager, and warehouse manager. The family continued to work full-time in the business.

LEFT PAGE: Bill on the crush pad which is now the Solera Patio next to the tasting room. INSET: Bill with friend Rusty Manning, and Mikey testing the alcohol levels. RIGHT PAGE: TOP: Craig and Libby with Carl, a retired Navy Seal who joined our staff early on. BOTTOM: Bill pouring in 2002.

MAKING WINE FUN

As a family, we strove to create the kind of winery we would want to visit. We had all experienced some California wineries that poured great wine but seemed aloof or pretentious. We wanted to take the wine off the *snob shelf* and make it fun. Realizing that people who visit wineries can feel insecure about their wine knowledge, we aimed to put our guests at ease.

Complex wine descriptions can be intimidating, so we paired our wine to experiences. For example, we told guests, "Our Angelica Cream Sherry pairs well with a warm mountain cabin in the middle of winter on a couch with your significant other in front of a crackling fire." We described our Riesling as a wine that "pairs well with poolsides, picnics, patios, and porch swings." Rosie made simple cork necklaces by gluing our used Champagne corks to a thin, gold ribbon. We would "cork" anyone who had a birthday or anniversary. We still honor that tradition today.

For our staff uniforms, Jenifer designed button-down, collared, short sleeve shirts that depicted our winery

building, hot air balloons, grapes, and multiple Golden Retrievers. Guests liked them so much that they insisted we make them available for sale. Over time, guests began visiting us proudly wearing their Wilson Creek "dog shirts."

At one of the valley-wide barrel tasting events at the winery, we wanted every visitor to try the Almond Champagne. So, we found a tool belt with two large leather pouches on each side, meant to hold a drill or nails. One of our female staff put a bottle of cold Almond in each pouch and walked around with plastic tumblers giving away free tastes. She poured through more than 50 bottles that day and became known as "The Almond Girl."

We also developed a chocolate port we called *Decadencia.* To a wine purist, adding chocolate to a port wine bordered on blasphemy. But the port already had chocolate tones to it, so we just added a tiny bit of natural chocolate. Deanna and I developed a partnership with Don Galleano, the patriarch of Galleano Winery, an hour north of us. He helped us a ton in those early years, and we bought some barrels of aged Zinfandel port from him. Filippi Winery helped with the chocolate formula and

LEFT PAGE: A trained monkey visited the winery and poured Almond Champagne for Rosie. He entertained guests by climbing on our gazebo. RIGHT PAGE: TOP: New Year's party in our event tent. MIDDLE LEFT: Staff helping in a barrel tasting event. Nicole (AKA "Almond Girl") with her tool belt to Libby's right. MIDDLE RIGHT: Bill and Libby. BOTTOM: Jazz musician Eric Darius performing at Wilson Creek.

bottled it for us. Deanna and I worked with Joey Filippi and tasted over 30 different types of chocolate percentages before landing on the final recipe. (I tasted through all of the samples, so Deanna drove me home that day). At Wilson Creek, we paired the chocolate port with Hershey's Kisses. Jenifer then discovered a chocolatier who produced shot glasses made of dark, Dutch chocolate. We began serving the Decadencia in those edible cups. They became so popular that we were soon the number-one buyer of the cups.

Our Decadencia Chocolate Port also paired well with a good cigar. Through a friend of Bill's, we teamed up with the Toraño Cigar Company and arranged to ship some of our port to Honduras where they rolled the cigars. There, the workers infused their premium tobacco leaves with our Decadencia Port. The result was a new and unique experience for cigar lovers. We held a release party at the winery to publicize the release of the *Reserva Decadencia* cigar. Carlos Toraño, the patriarch and owner, flew from Miami to attend. We hired a cigar roller who made fresh cigars on the spot for our guests. Rosie even got behind the table and rolled some with his help.

We held more such events that were not typical for a winery: a crawfish boil, a '70s party, Super Bowl parties, and other themed events. For one New Year's party, we chose the theme *Arabian Nights* and brought in a live camel that guests could pose with for photos.

We wanted our winery grounds to have a parklike feel, to be a place where people could unwind. We built a playground to make the winery kid-friendly, and where parents could enjoy a glass of wine as they watched their children.

Music was an essential part of the experience too. To enhance the family vibe, we played contemporary jazz and classic rock throughout the property. I used a five-CD changer as our primary sound system, although I often had to battle with one of our wine servers who would sneak in his heavy metal CDs. I told him that although I loved hard rock as well, we needed music that would appeal to most of the guests. So, I replaced *Metallica* and *AC/DC* with *Dave Koz* and the *Eagles*.

MAKING WINE TOO FUN?

Word spread throughout Temecula Valley Wine Country about Wilson Creek: it was a fun winery, an approachable family, and a great place to visit. The downside was that a few of the other wineries labeled us "the party winery."

In those days, it was customary for wineries to host inter-winery tastings, where they could introduce their wines to the staff of other wineries. These were typically small gatherings involving about 20 guests. When our turn to host one came, we decided to do things differently. We approached it the way we had handled such events going back to our days in South Pasadena—we invited everyone and threw a big party. We put a flyer together and passed it out to all the other wineries.

We also decided to add a theme and make it a toga party. We even tracked down Otis Day and The Knights—the band featured in the movie *Animal House*—and hired them to perform live.

We didn't want to be known as "the Animal House winery" (even though Gerry, Bill, and I had all been fraternity presidents), but we did want a fun party. When the day rolled around, more than 450 winery employees and friends showed up. Most dressed in colorful togas, many of them homemade. Otis Day rocked the night, capping the evening with a lively rendition of "Shout!"

The visitors from the other wineries quickly learned that we were fun—*and* that we had some excellent wines. But, unfortunately, this event helped further the "party winery" reputation.

A few wine country residents felt the party ambiance conflicted with the region's prestigious image and took their grievances to the newspapers. Bill read a quote that particularly frustrated him: "We don't want Temecula Wine Country to become the Disneyland of wine regions." Bill wrestled with how to respond to these complaints.

LEFT PAGE TOP: Our "Arabian Nights" New Year's party. MIDDLE: A Super Bowl party in our event tent. BOTTOM: Rosie rolling a cigar at the release of our Reserva Decadencia Cigar. RIGHT PAGE: The inter-winery toga party with Otis Day and the Knights *on the stage. Can you spot Jenifer, Bill and Libby?*

100

2019 event

"The fun dynamic is what sets us apart."

Bill was president of the *2020 Wine Country Plan* which had worked hard to come up with a proposal for the future of the area. His role was to present the 2020 plan to the Riverside County Board of Supervisors for approval. With the article he'd read a week earlier still in his mind, Bill readied his presentation.

The day of the supervisors' meeting arrived. The large assembly room was packed with reporters and concerned residents, as this 2020 plan was *the* proposal for the future of wine country.

Bill stood at the mic in front of the supervisors and the restless crowd. Then he reached into a bag he'd brought. He came up with a winery baseball hat, which he put on his head. "I wear many hats," he began. "I am a business owner who wants my business to thrive." He took off the hat and replaced it with a cowboy hat. "I am also a farmer who wants the healthiest grapes possible."

He had everyone's attention.

He put on an orange hardhat and said, "I am also concerned for the air quality in wine country, so I stand opposed to the rock quarry that is proposed to go in just west of our valley."

He then reached into his bag and put on a hat that caused dozens of cameras to flash.

"I wear these Mickey Mouse ears because I just read a book called *The Disney Way*. We should be proud to be called the 'Disneyland of wineries.' The Disney properties are well run and known to be the happiest places on earth. Their amusement parks are fun and have something for everyone. Disney has excellent customer service, cleanliness, and good management practices. Like Disney, Temecula Valley Wine Country has so much to offer to so many! We offer a wide variety of activities for both residents and visitors. We want this wine region to be enjoyable. That's why we have all types of wineries, balloon companies, golf courses, hotels, and restaurants. So, let's embrace being the "Disneyland of wineries!"

His clever stunt prompted the reporters to take lots of pictures and merited an article in a regional newspaper, *The Press-Enterprise*.

We realized that being the party winery could alienate guests who wanted to experience fantastic wines in a relaxing setting. So, we worked to replace the party label with "fun" and "entertaining." There are a ton of classy wineries in California with great wine and upscale atmosphere. We strive for those elements too, but the fun dynamic is what sets us apart.

104

LEFT PAGE: Bill refereeing a golf cart polo match next to our vines. BOTTOM: Bill driving a group on a vineyard tour.
RIGHT PAGE: TOP: Bill at the supervisors' hearing. BOTTOM: Craig presenting a custom labeled bottle to "Thunder" at the Lake Elsinore Storm Baseball Stadium.

THE "OFFICIAL" WINERY OF THE NAVY

Shortly after we opened in 2000, two gentlemen visited Wilson Creek and tasted our wines. Afterward, they approached Rosie and introduced themselves as naval commanders from the aircraft carrier USS Constellation (CV-64) based in San Diego (Naval Air Station North Island). Dressed in civilian clothes, these men were the ship's executive officer (XO) and supply officer (SUPPO), respectively. They asked Rosie, "Do you do private labels on your wines?"

She wasn't sure how to answer, so she consulted Bill and me. We looked at each other and shrugged, "Sure." We had never done such a thing but figured we could make it happen somehow. We both chatted with the commanders. The executive officer told us, "I tell you what. I'll hook

you up with our ship's design department. What we're looking for is something we can call 'Captain's Private Reserve.' It doesn't come out of taxpayer's money, because each officer pays into the officers' mess fund for better food and entertainment. When we're on deployment and pull into a foreign port, heads of state come aboard the carrier to dine with the captain, and all the dignitaries will enjoy your wine. So, hopefully, this wine will travel all over the world, wherever our carrier battle group goes."

I drove to the supply officer's home in Coronado. I took two bottles of each of our wines for the other officers to taste. At the supply officer's home, a dozen naval officers sampled the wines and selected the Sangiovese. Then the graphic artists on the USS

Constellation drew up a couple of label designs. But the commanding officer had an idea of his own. On a paper napkin, he sketched an airplane taking off from a carrier, depicting the way a plane dips in the air immediately after the steam catapult shoots it off the bow of the ship. That became our design.

We printed the labels, and our softball team applied them to the bottles by hand. Soon, Gerry and I were driving 1,000 bottles of wine to Naval Air Station North Island with our reliable old Mazda minivan and its 5'x7' trailer. We arrived at the base at night. The guard at the gate directed us to the carrier, which stood 13 stories high. It was so huge that at first, we mistook it for a giant building. Five sailors offloaded the wine for us.

The next day we got a phone call. "Hello," a voice said, "this is the aircraft carrier, USS John C. Stennis. We received a bottle from the XO of the USS Constellation docked next to us. So, where's *our* wine?" Word of our special-label wines had spread from ship to ship—without an ounce of advertising on our part. We produced a custom label for the John C. Stennis. After we delivered the wine to them, other aircraft carriers started contacting us.

The aircraft carriers used the wine for gift exchanges with ships from other countries, including France and the United Kingdom. When the John C. Stennis (CVN-74) docked in Hobart, Tasmania, the officers traded wines with their counterparts from the Charles de Gaulle (R91), a French carrier. Their commanding officer reportedly loved our wine.

106

TOP: Mick and Bill on "Vulture's Row" on board the USS Nimitz (CVN-68). INSET: The first Navy label we did. "South Coast" is the larger region that includes Temecula Valley and San Diego.

The commanding officer of the USS Constellation thanked us by flying Gerry, Rosie, Christopher, and me onto the carrier while they were at sea on maneuvers. We took off from the base in Coronado in a *Carrier Onboard Delivery* (COD) plane. As the plane touched down on the flight deck, its tailhook grabbed one of the arresting wires, which decelerates the aircraft from 120 miles per hour to a violent stop in two seconds. I felt as if all my internal organs slammed against my ribs. We spent the next 24 hours on board, receiving the distinguished visitor (DV) treatment. We had dinner with the captain, and Rosie and Gerry slept in the captain's guest quarters. The next day we launched off the carrier. The ship's steam catapults accelerated us from zero to 130 miles per hour in two seconds.

I came home and described our incredible aircraft carrier experience to Bill. I could tell he didn't quite believe me, but a year later, he got to experience it for himself. The nuclear carrier USS Nimitz (CVN-68) was conducting maneuvers off the San Diego coast to prepare the air wing for deployment to the Persian Gulf. And the commanding officer invited us aboard. Bill and I went with Mikey, our winemaker, and Bill's friend Rusty, who is a balloon pilot. We got tail-hooked, as before, and then toured the carrier. We spent some time on *Vulture's Row,* a small balcony high above the flight deck, where we watched the F/A-18F Super Hornet planes land and take off. It takes a lot to impress Bill, but for 45 minutes, we all watched the intricate choreography of practice landings and aircraft moving on deck within inches of each other. We all wore ear protection so we couldn't talk without yelling. Bill looked at me and mouthed, "Wow." We spent time with the landing signal officer (LSO) watching night landings right next to the flight deck and hung out with the renowned Strike Fighter Squadron 41, *The Black Aces* (VFA-41). We eventually made a custom wine label for them, as well.

We still have a great relationship with the Navy in Coronado, as they refer to us as "unofficially, the official winery of the U.S. Navy." It's been my privilege to serve as the winery's liaison to the Navy. Over the years, I learned that each officer has an "O" to designate *officer* after his or her title. For example,

the commanding officer is CO, the supply officer is SUP-PO, the executive officer is XO, the aircraft maintenance officer is FIXO, etc. Some officers gave me the "official" title, WINE-O.

For more than ten years, we've had the honor of hosting the Third Fleet's Annual Sailor of the Year event at the winery. Our tasting room has an Honor Wall with photos of some of the ships and military units for whom we've bottled and labeled wine: USS Nimitz (CVN-68), USS Constellation (CV-64), USS Ronald Reagan (CVN-73), USS John C. Stennis (CVN-74), USS Peleliu (LHA-5), USS Theodore Roosevelt (CVN-71), USS Carl Vinson (CVN-70), and many others. We have also produced custom labels for the U.S. Army (General Tommy Franks), Marines, Navy Seals, Air Force generals, and Coast Guard.

We even did a custom label for President George W. Bush, and for the White House Chief of Staff in 2016.

For me, developing these relationships with the Navy and other branches of our military has been one of the highlights of representing Wilson Creek.

LEFT PAGE: TOP: Bill with friend Rusty Manning (on his right) and winemaker Mike Calabro.
BOTTOM: The "Honor Wall" in our tasting room with photos of the Navy ships as well as various Air Force, Army and Marine labels.
RIGHT PAGE: A sampling of the Navy labels we have done.

WILSON CREEK AWARDS

2001 - 2004 - 2007 - 2010
Temecula Valley Chamber of Commerce
Business of the Year

2006
People's Choice Award – Chula Vista Rotary

2009
People's Choice Award
Temecula Balloon and Wine Festival
Best of Southern California Meetings and
Events

2010
Spirit of Entrepreneur Award – Bill Wilson
Citizen of the Year – Bill Wilson
Best of San Diego Award – Union Tribune
Best of Southern California
Meetings and Events
Best Winery in the Inland Empire,
Inland Empire Magazine
Lifetime Achievement Award
Rosie & Gerry Wilson

2011
Best of Southern California
Meetings and Events
Best Winery in the Inland Empire,
Inland Empire Magazine

2012
Reader's Choice Award – Press Enterprise
Best Winery in the Inland Empire,
Inland Empire Magazine
Award of Excellence – Wine Spectator
Award of Excellence – Trip Advisor

2013
Best Winery in the Inland Empire,
Inland Empire Magazine
Xenia – Welty Award Tourism Professional
of the Year – Bill Wilson

2014
Reader's Choice Award – Press Enterprise
Best Winery in the Inland Empire,
Inland Empire Magazine

2015
Xenia Cilurzo Award – Winery of the Year
Best Winery in the Inland Empire,
Inland Empire Magazine
Award of Excellence – Trip Advisor
Xenia Social Media Award

109

THE FRUIT OF GENEROSITY

Wilson Creek had been open for just over a year when we won the prestigious Temecula Valley Chamber of Commerce *Gold Business of the Year* in 2001, an award given to the business that has the most philanthropic and community impact. Rosie was stunned. "I couldn't believe it," she said. "That came right out of the blue."

I think we won because Rosie and Gerry have always been generous and involved in their community. While in Minnesota, Gerry led the county Republican Party as the president, served in Kiwanis and on the school board, and raised funds for Multiple Sclerosis research. In South Pasadena, he attended Rotary in L.A., served as president of the local Little League, and was chairman of the church board. Rosie volunteered numerous hours cooking for her church and helped neighbors whenever they needed a hot meal or a hug.

When we came to Temecula, the whole family kept doing what Rosie and Gerry had always done—joyfully serving others. We kids absorbed their giving attitude and became involved in the community. We donated wine to multiple nonprofit organizations and took every opportunity to pour at fundraising events. From 2000 to 2001, we served our wines at over 200 charity events. In

that first year, we poured or donated outright approximately 800 cases. Our motives were mixed; we truly loved helping others but also needed to get our name out there. We quickly learned that one of the best ways to promote our brand was to have a family member pour at an event.

After receiving the *Gold Business of the Year* award, Gerry comments, "Maybe it was because we were the first part of the 'second wave' of wineries. We were the 14th winery. Those who went before us were pioneers who started Temecula Valley Wine Country. They laid the foundation for people like us to follow. When the entire Wilson family arrived, some of them thought, *Who are these guys*? Many wineries embraced us, but some viewed us as outsiders who didn't have a clue. In many ways they were correct."

LEFT PAGE: 2001 Business of the Year event.
RIGHT PAGE: TOP: 2010 Business of the Year event.
BOTTOM: 2015 Chamber Awards Gala.

Some wineries loved our presence, reminding us that "Visitors have to drive by us to get to you." And, as the saying goes, *all boats rise with the tide.*

"Local wineries and businesses started to recognize that we brought a whole new culture to Temecula Wine Country," Gerry says. "The existing wineries were doing fine before us, but I think we brought in a passion for genuine hospitality. We hopefully brought a level of kindness and sincerity to guests. Over time, guests feel like they are visiting our family home, not just our family business."

Rosie adds, "Yes, in those early years, the property served as the home to three Wilson families. So, we were welcoming people into our lives. Gerry and I would invite people to our home for wine and cheese. Bill and Jenifer were at the winery constantly, connecting with people. Mick and Deanna served at the bar nearly every day. Craig and Libby poured at numer-

2016
People's Choice Award (2012 Petite Sirah)
Temecula Valley Winegrowers Association
Best Winery in the Inland Empire,
Inland Empire Magazine
Best Winery Award - Press-Enterprise

2017
Wedding Wire Couples' Choice
Best of Inland Empire,
Inland Empire Magazine
Best Winery in the Inland Empire,
Inland Empire Magazine
Best Winery – SoCal Life in Lux
Community Leader Award – Rosie Wilson

2018
Wedding Wire Couples' Choice
Los Angeles Travel Magazine Best Winery
Best Winery in the Inland Empire,
Inland Empire Magazine
Xenia Social Media Award
Xenia Ambassador Award

2019
Best Winery in the Inland Empire,
Inland Empire Magazine

2020
Wedding Wire Couples' Choice

Gerry Wilson

is the dad of the Wilson family of Wilson Creek Winery in Temecula, California. He is the father of four adult children and grandfather of seven.

Gerry was born in Montana, but shortly after that his family moved to Minneapolis, Minnesota where he spent his formative years, including many years as a Boy Scout.

Gerry and his bride of 55 years, Rosie can be seen most days at the Winery. While Gerry and Rosie had been looking forward to retirement, when the idea came to open up a "small, family business," everyone pitched in everything they had to build a new business, a new life, a new world for the whole family.

Wilson Creek Winery and the Wilson's are known for their many contributions to the community including Special Olympics, American Diabetes Association, Y.M.C.A., Temecula Valley Chamber of Commerce, Temecula Valley Convention and Visitors Bureau, and the Temecula Valley Balloon and Wine Festival. The result of everyone's effort was having Wilson Creek Winery voted the 2007 Temecula Valley Gold Business of the Year.

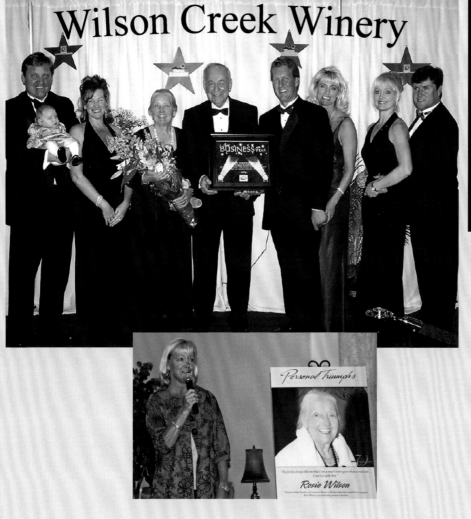

Wilson Creek Winery

LEFT PAGE: TOP: Gerry receiving The Father of the Year award in San Diego RIGHT: The announcement from The Boy Scouts of America, Tahquitz District where they awarded Gerry the 2008 Distinguished Citizen Award. BOTTOM: LEFT: 2001 Business of the Year gala. RIGHT: Bill with the Riverside County 2010 Spirit of the Entrepreneur Award. BOTTOM: Libby honoring Rosie at the Personal Triumphs awards.

ous offsite charity events, as well as in the tasting room. People sensed the family hospitality and responded to it."

Bill says, "If the Wilson family moved to Texas or Timbuktu, it'd be the same thing. It wouldn't be a strategy; it would be who we are; we would start loving people. With the winery, all of a sudden the business is the vehicle for that love. I think that's what has helped Wilson Creek succeed—people picked up on that vibe."

We won the *Gold Business of the Year* again in 2004. As the announcer described the ways our family had served the community, I felt awestruck. We were making an impact.

Gerry and Rosie received a *Lifetime Achievement Award* at the same Temecula Valley Chamber of Commerce Gala in 2010. In a little over a decade, they became two of the most influential people in the valley—not in terms of power or wealth, but in impacting lives and the community as a whole. Bill also won *Citizen of the Year* in 2010, at the same gala. We actually felt a little embarrassed that we were so prominently represented.

Bill won the Riverside County *Entrepreneur of the Year* in 2010. This award is given to the top entrepreneur in the entire Inland Empire. It was well-deserved recognition for Bill's efforts in starting and growing the winery.

SOME OF OUR WINE AWARDS

6 Wine Enthusiast
Rated 90+ and above

27 Wine Enthusiast
Rated 80+ and above

4 "Best of Class"

5 "Chairman's Awards"

52 Gold Medals

81 Silver Medals

90 Bronze Medals

"*The people of Temecula have been very kind to us, so we want to give back.
We love to be generous, as giving is in our DNA.*" - Rosie Wilson

113   TOP: *The Juvenile Diabetes Research Foundation "Walk for the Cure" in our vineyards. BOTTOM: The Special Olympics "Torch Run"
that starts at Pechanga and ends at the winery. Merlot is escorting the final runner. The run is sponsored by local law enforcement.*

TOP: Bill coming with presents at "Jacob's Gift" which we host annually to benefit special needs kids.
BOTTOM: The annual Easter egg hunt that we do for the staff and their families every year.

IVCC

TEMECULA VALLEY CHAMBER OF COMMERCE

TEMECULA
Today!

JULY 2002

Volume 28 • Number 7

The Wilson Family—
Following Their Dream

City News

Dining Guide

Commentary —
County's Blueprint
Preserves Local Control

This article, from *Temecula Today*, July 2002, sums up the moment:

THE WILSON FAMILY - FOLLOWING THEIR DREAM   by Karen Roberts

There is a mantra in the Wilson family. Rosie Wilson sums it up with one word, "tenacity," other family members call it "passion." The Wilson family has funneled their tenacity and passion into the creation of the award-winning Wilson Creek Winery and into service for their community.

When they were nominated for Temecula Valley Chamber of Commerce 2001 Gold Business of the Year, Rosie's children told her that she would have to shuck her denims and tennis shoes and buy a long dress, heels, and some "sparkling" earrings to replace her grape earrings.

"I was sure that there was no way we would win," said Rosie. "We were so new, I didn't even hear our name called when it was announced, but I looked up, and there was Wilson Creek Winery on the screen. I stood up and whooped, and the whole audience stood and whooped," she smiled. "That was worth the award itself."

When asked what was the key to winning the award, Rosie grinned, "We were asked to fill out on a half-page what community organizations and events we had been involved in during the past year. We were surprised that by the time we went through our calendar, we had a single-spaced list 15 pages long. The community has given so much to us; we want to give back."

"We enjoyed wine, but we knew nothing about operating a winery," said Gerry. "We took a few classes, read a lot of books, and asked for advice. The area wineries were a great resource. They gave us a lot of good advice and helped us when we needed it."

On October 14, 2000, Wilson Creek Winery opened its doors. It was a double celebration because Rosie had also turned 70. From 2,000 cases of wine the first year to 15,000 cases the second year, and over 150 weddings, the Wilson family has had a champagne coming out. Their Wine Club boasts over 2,200 members, and this year alone, their wine has earned over 20 awards.

"I'm the luckiest man in the world," Gerry smiled. "My family is all here. I have spectacular sunsets, the stars at night and the hot air balloons in the day."

"Anyone can buy wine at a store," said Gerry. "When people visit our winery, we want them to have a wine experience. We want them to feel as if they've been welcomed into our home -- in fact, they have been." Most of the Wilsons live on the property.

Visiting the winery is an authentic family experience. Visitors meet the Wilson family, including their grandchildren, as well as Max, Taffy, and Merlot, their dogs. "People visit and ask where the dogs are," chuckled Rosie.

Their work is a family affair, and Wine Club members become the extended Wilson family.

"It's a synergistic effect," said Mick. "We all have strong personalities, and when you put all the ideas together, you have a much better result. This is an evolving project."

The Wilsons have many hats. Rosie makes all the staff lunch every day, works in the tasting room, and she cares for the flowers. Gerry's the detail person; he handles the finances, works in the tasting room, and makes sure the bathrooms are in excellent condition. Gerry leaned forward, "People judge you by your bathrooms."

"You have to follow your passion," said Bill. "If you work toward your dream, things will happen. If you aren't following your passion, but just working for the money, you'll never achieve your dream. So, what do you have?"

When they were both 70, they went skydiving in Lake Elsinore. After the experience Gerry casually mentioned it to his doctor who replied, "Gerry, you did what? No, No. I love that you are adventurous, but promise me you will never skydive again." Gerry agreed. A few months later Rosie dove on two separate occasions — the second time with Mick, Deanna and a few Wine Club members.

Hayden and Gavin helping.

GROWING PAINS

As we continued to grow, we ran out of space for wine tasting and events. We bought some used office trailers, including one 40-footer that we converted into a restroom facility—consisting of two restrooms with four stalls each. For our events, we purchased two large canvas event tents. These large tents served us for years, but they had some drawbacks.

One day we were hosting the officers from the USS Stennis in our large event tent when a fierce windstorm hit. The weather experts called it a *vortex*—a rare combination of currents that create a massive burst of wind. It was raining hard when the 80-mile-per-hour winds arrived. The tent was tied down, but everyone evacuated and went into the tasting room for shelter—except Bill. He wasn't going to let some freak storm ruin his tent, so he and a few others held on to one corner as the wind tossed the tent walls around like loose sails on a ship.

A large amount of water had collected in the sagging canvas above their heads. I ran out and yelled at Bill, "Hey, get your tail inside. That tent is not worth your life!" He couldn't hear me over the wind's roar. At that time a big gust caught the tent corner and tossed Bill and the others tending it eight feet in the air.

As they all got up and ran inside, they glanced behind to witness the tent corner collapse, releasing a massive deluge of water where they had been standing.

LEFT PAGE: TOP: A micro-burst wine storm demolished a cabana and damaged the event tent. MIDDLE: The same wind storm snapped a large tree in our lower garden. BOTTOM: Flood in 2019. RIGHT PAGE: 2017 snow.

BUGS AND WEATHER

By 2002 we were even busier, and our future looked bright. Then one day our vineyard manager informed us we had a problem with a tiny insect called the glassy-winged sharpshooter. The importance of this news was slow to dawn on most of us. But Rosie's family roots are in farming, so she knew well how small creatures could cause significant damage. We soon learned that this bug had the potential to wipe out most of Temecula's vines. The bad news made for a depressing day.

After we had struggled to build our winery and spent every penny we had, we felt we were finally getting back on our feet. And now the experts told us we faced the prospect of losing most, if not all, of our vines.

The sharpshooter feeds on vines and spreads Pierce's Disease (PD) through its saliva. Once a vine contracts PD, it dies within two years. This tiny insect had migrated from Florida and worked its way to Temecula. Regional agencies were doing what they could to fight the infestation. But when the sharpshooter started migrating north to the wine regions of Santa Barbara and the Central Coast, the county, state, and federal governments got involved. They spent millions of dollars researching and developing solutions. The acclaimed wine departments at the University of California, Davis, and California State University, Fresno joined in the fight.

Temecula became ground zero for the infestation in California. Experts knew that what happened here would affect the entire state. They did everything to eradicate the bug and keep it contained in Southern California. Temecula vineyards even received a per-acre government incentive to rip out the infected vines. Most winegrowers realized the gravity of the risk and complied. Before it was over, they had removed hundreds of acres of vines. The growers worked with the experts to create a pesticide that killed the bugs as they fed on the leaves. Within two years, growers replanted most of the acreage.

The disease forced us to replant a few acres of white grapes. Thankfully, our old vines of Cabernet and Zinfandel proved to be resilient. We tested our vines individually and replanted those found to be diseased.

In the end, we lost about 20 percent of our vines—far less than the 80 to 95 percent some had predicted. And, thanks to the various agencies working together, California's wine industry survived the plague of the sharpshooters. Still today, we are all collectively working to find a cure and plant vines that are resistant to the disease.

Insects were only one of the threats we had to face. In our first five years, we endured flooding, frost, hail, snow, scorching heat waves, the threat of a nearby wildfire, vine diseases, and nasty winds.

Welcome to farming, where threats to the crop are the nature of the beast. The learning curve was steep, but we figured it out one crisis at a time.

Welcome to farming, where threats to the crop are the nature of the beast.
The learning curve was steep, but we figured it out one crisis at a time.

CABERNET SAUVIGNON

THE BEGINNING OF THE

121 *"Extended Family" Wine Club*

THE WINE CLUB

Be it Minnesota or South Pasadena, our family created
an extended family of friends and neighbors wherever
we lived. So, it was only natural for those who loved our
winery to think of themselves as part of an extended
family. Many asked us to start a wine club. We realized
they wanted to be a part of what we were doing. So, we
launched the *Extended Family* Wine Club. Within the
first two months, hundreds joined. Each member received
two bottles, deeply discounted, shipped to their house
every other month. Members also liked the fact that they
could have free tastings every time they visited the winery.

A few months after we launched the club, we started
to take a Polaroid photo of each new Wine Club member
and mounted it next to the large Wilson family photo
on the wall behind the tasting room bar. We wrote each
member's name on the photo with a Sharpie and taped
it next to the large picture frame. Over the ensuing
weeks, more new members wanted their photos there as
well. Soon, hundreds of Polaroids surrounded the family
picture. The club grew so fast that we had to start taping
photos on the hallway walls. Within six months, photos
filled a long 12-foot wall. Then, a few months later, the
opposite wall filled too—creating a tunnel of photos.

LEFT PAGE TOP: Wine Club members pointing to their photos.
BOTTOM: The beginning of the Wine Club photo wall.
RIGHT PAGE: TOP: Gerry with members.
BOTTOM: Wine Club grape stomping party.

124

ALMOND CHAMPAGNE GROWS

The demand for our Almond Champagne continued to increase. Soon, local stores and restaurants were asking for it. Deanna, who had sales management experience, oversaw our distribution. Almond Champagne soon began appearing in supermarkets, resorts, wedding facilities, and restaurants.

We bought a delivery truck and hired a driver. In 2004, Deanna hired a dynamic sales representative named Chuck Spiegel. We soon were in 15 states in the southwest. In partnership with some large distributor companies, Chuck added 20 more states.

The family also continued to pour Almond Champagne wherever we could, along with our other wines. But now, when people tasted it, we could also tell them where to buy it.

One 2005 story exemplifies the Almond effect. Bill drove to one such event with Chuck, who was hired to grow our distribution. On the way, Bill told Chuck, "I know you'll think I'm nuts for bringing all these cases, but watch how this event unfolds. It happens every time. We'll start slow, but once everybody starts telling others about what we have, there'll be a line for the Almond Champagne."

Chuck assumed Bill was exaggerating. Chuck recalls, "I've never seen anything like it! It did start slow, and then suddenly we had a huge line—the entire day!

Toward the end of the event, the vendor pouring next to us was reading a magazine, and Bill and I were frantically both pouring Almond Champagne with a bottle in each hand."

Bill echoes that observation. "Sure enough, at each of these events we attend, people ask, 'Are you the one with the Almond?' Within an hour, we have the longest line of the event. Doing these charity events has been key to our success. Sometimes I feel like a drug dealer—I have people taste it and get them hooked."

Years later, whenever we showed guests around the property, we would say, "This is the winepress that Almond bought!" "This is the truck that Almond purchased!" "This is the large event tent that Almond obtained!" "These are my daughter's shoes that Almond got for us." It is amazing that a sparkling wine with the flavor of a nut is what brought us our initial success.

TOP: Chuck, our VP of Sales with our "fleet" of three vehicles. LOWER: Deanna and Mick pouring at a fundraising event.
RIGHT PAGE: Our label from 2004-2016.

2003

FAMILY TENSION

Family businesses often fail because of internal divisions. It can be easy for families to get along when the individuals only see each other occasionally. But when they work together every day, as our family does, sparks can fly.

As our business grew, the family issues we had swept under the carpet began to surface. And the more we worked together, the more the tensions were magnified. The conflict especially grieved Gerry and Rosie. Their vision for the winery was to reunify the family. Now it seemed to be pulling us apart.

Bill puts it this way: "The good news is that I am in business with my family. And the bad news is that I am in business with my family!"

We learned that as the business grew, it was important for the family to get along. There were disputes about who was entitled to what and who had the authority to do what. Some felt Bill was treating the winery as his own

company. After all, he was the one with the vision, and he had worked extremely hard to get the winery open. But others felt they were no less committed. As far as other family members were concerned, it was a family enterprise, not a sole proprietorship called "Bill Wilson Creek."

Family board meetings became increasingly tense. Conflict escalated. We recognized we needed outside expertise—a professional mediator who knew how to work with family businesses. We found a good one, Kent Rhodes, who helped us communicate as a family and establish common goals. He began by interviewing the family members individually and helping to mediate our family board meetings. He also met with the key staff managers to get their perspectives.

Kent forced us to address tense family issues. We suddenly had to be brutally honest with each other, and it was sometimes overwhelming. For example, I felt that

TOP ROW: LEFT TO RIGHT: Craig, Hayden, Libby, Bill, Jenifer, Deanna, Mick.
BOTTOM ROW: LEFT TO RIGHT: Gerry, Cassidy, Rosie, Cambria, Gavin.

Bill was disregarding my input. I would offer feedback on what projects we should do or what wines we should sell, and he would ignore it. I eventually grew so frustrated that I slowly distanced myself from the business. But Kent had been observing the family members and noting how each family member was wired differently. He pulled me aside and told me that my gift mix was needed to counterbalance Bill's. He encouraged me to get back into the game.

I began to appreciate how Bill and I complement each other. As brothers, we've always been close. But we are total opposites. He initiates things; I organize them. I tend to ask "Why?" and, "How?" Bill says, "Why not?" Bill is an entrepreneur; I'm a stabilizer. I think of Bill as the one hacking his way through the jungle with a machete, while I'm behind him cleaning up all the branches and asking, "Where are we going? Are you sure this is the right way?"

"Bill is the entrepreneur," Gerry says. "And he's the driving force behind the winery. Mick, being the middle child, is wired differently and is more systems-oriented. He's more of the check-and-balance person. You need both."

The family business consultant observed, "When the two of you work together, it is a powerful combination, as you complement one another. When you disregard the perspective of the other you lose out on the beauty of the opposite viewpoint. I've never seen such potential in two people—if you learn to work better together."

I've learned that I can't change Bill. But I can accept him for who he is and be thankful for his strengths. Without him, there would be no winery. He is truly the face of Wilson Creek. He is highly involved, and most people in the area know Bill. When he walks into a room, he brings energy and passion. Our staff came up with the acronym, FOB, as so many people who visit us say they are *friends of Bill's*. Why would I want to change that?

Gerry puts the family conflict into perspective: "When you have a family operation, everybody comes along with a certain amount of baggage. The name of the game is to try to get everybody in a place or in a position that they enjoy. It has been difficult, but so far, we've been relatively successful at that."

WE NEED MORE LAND!

In 2002, we learned that the landowners who sold us our original 20 acres were willing to sell us another 20-acre parcel. We knew we needed more land. And if we didn't buy it, another winery could build right next door. So, we borrowed more money and bought the parcel. We did this twice more over the next four years. It felt as if we were playing Monopoly, buying up land whenever we could. Eventually, we ended up with 96 acres—a huge spread for suburbanites like us. Now we were able to plant more vines and produce more wine to meet the growing demand.

2019

BOTTOM: Christopher driving one of the tractors during harvest.

WILSON CREEK GOES HOLLYWOOD

Television and film producers began taking note of Wilson Creek. It started in 2002 with a documentary TV series called *Radical Sabbatical*, which chronicled the experiences of people who left their ordinary lives to pursue dreams of adventure. The producers had heard of the winery—and of Bill and Jenifer, who were natural subjects for such a show. We agreed to have the producers come and shoot an episode. They sent a camera crew and spent three days filming. The resulting show aired a few times and was later picked up by a major airline, which featured it on numerous flights. People visited the winery based on that show and treated us like celebrities.

The Oprah Winfrey Show shot a segment about Wilson Creek, but it got bumped and never aired. Reality show producers approached us four different

times, wanting to feature our family. After wrestling with that idea, we agreed to participate in one. But after a week of filming, it became apparent they were only interested in highlighting our family conflicts, so we pulled the plug.

Bill recalls, "We have been featured on numerous reality shows. We hosted *Blind Date* and *Family Jewels* with Gene Simmons, to name a few. It's an honor to have someone use your facility for their show. It's fun to see what they create as the finished product. We couldn't believe how much was left on the editing floor though."

Prominent people from all walks of life also began to discover Wilson Creek, including NFL stars, NBA greats, actors, and producers. Such visits became a normal part of life at Wilson Creek.

TOP TO BOTTOM: Filming for a segment on Oprah. Craig and Libby with President George Bush. Jenifer, Libby and Craig with Arnold at a fundraiser.

TOP TO BOTTOM: Jenifer with Celine Dion and friends Cherise Manning (on left) and Christin Powers. Bill with Paula Dean at an 134
event. Filming for a segment on Oprah. The crew spent three days at the winery filming, but unfortunately the episode never aired. Jenifer
with Gene Simmons of the rock group KISS *when he filmed a segment at the winery for his show,* Family Jewels. *Craig and Libby with*
Congresswoman Mary Bono Mack.

LAWYERS—UGH!

We kids wanted to name a wine to honor Rosie and Gerry. We brainstormed as a family, and everyone liked the name *Legacy,* as it captured what Rosie and Gerry were creating. I did a quick trademark search and assumed the name was okay to use. We produced our Legacy wine in 2004, a "Bordeaux blend" of Merlot, Cabernet Sauvignon, Cabernet Franc, and Malbec. We only sold it in the tasting room and to our Wine Club members.

But we soon learned that our growth had put us on the radar of other wineries. We received a "cease and desist" letter from the law firm of a very large winery, claiming they owned the mark for Legacy. We agreed to immediately stop production under the Legacy label. We changed the name to *Meritage*—the term used in the United States for a Bordeaux blend (*Meritage* is a combination of *merit* and *heritage,* and rhymes with *heritage.*) What we couldn't change was the tall, ten-foot bottle sculpture displayed in the courtyard with the Legacy label carved out of sheet metal.

That wasn't our last encounter with big corporate lawyers. Some of our wine servers started creating sparkling wine cocktails for guests. One of the favorites that emerged was the Almond Champagne with a tad of Decadencia Chocolate Port added. It had hints of both almond and chocolate, so we informally called it "Almond Joy." The name was only mentioned on our tasting menus and in our online newsletter. But it caught the eye of a law firm representing a large candy company, and we received another "cease and desist or we will sue you" letter. Of course, we immediately complied, and our Wine Club members helped us come up with another name: *Chocolate Almond-tini.* It's not as good as the original, but we don't have a lawsuit on our hands.

Former winemaker, Etienne Cowper, testing the Yes, Dear *Chardonnay.*

YES, DEAR

From 2000 to 2005 we produced a Chardonnay that was relatively high in acidity and lightly oaked. Jenifer fell in love with some more buttery and oaky Chardonnay wines from Napa. She and her friends were buying those wines because our Chardonnay was too tart for her. So, one day in 2006, she asked Bill, "Could you have our wine-maker make a Chardonnay that is more buttery and oaky?" Bill's thoughtful response was, "Yes, dear!" The following year the *Yes, Dear* Chardon-nay became a hit and soon replaced our more tart Chardonnay. We still produce our *Yes, Dear* every year. As a tradition, Jenifer has to taste the wine to give her ceremonial thumbs-up before we bottle it. We also renamed our Chardonnay vineyard, "Happy Wife" vineyard.

We rented a large crane to move the concert stage to make room to build a larger concert stage. On the left, Bill is holding a corner post to keep the structure from swaying. After the stage was secure Bill surprised us all by swinging while just holding the straps. Thankfully OSHA was not there that day.

JAZZING UP WILSON CREEK

After the winery opened, Bill knew that the large courtyard area we had created would be an excellent venue for concerts. A few other area wineries were hosting concerts, which we enjoyed attending. But we wanted to do it the Wilson way. Bill contacted the manager of a popular jazz artist who came to the winery and met with Bill and me. We showed him the open courtyard area that could seat 500. The manager asked where the band would play. Bill pointed to the wedding gazebo. We had already had some local bands play there, and it seemed to work fine. The manager laughed. "Um," he said, "that gazebo will only hold the drum set."

In short, if we wanted to host large concerts, we'd need a much bigger stage.

We worked with our architect to design and build a concert stage. This new concert venue became the setting for our *Sunset in the Vines* jazz series. During the next five years, we were able to host such jazz luminaries as Warren Hill, Norman Brown, Jeff Golub, Nick Colionne, Dave Koz, and Andre Delano.

As the concert crowds grew over the next two years, Bill sensed that we needed an even larger concert stage, which meant we needed to move the existing stage. We rented a large crane to move the stage to the other side of the courtyard. It was quite a sight, seeing Bill riding on top of the entire structure as the massive crane lifted it into the air and across the property. I'm thankful no government safety inspectors were there that day. We then built a larger concert stage where the smaller one was.

In 2012, our focus shifted to country music. We knew these concerts would be popular, but we had no idea so many country fans lived in and around Temecula. Most of the shows sold out. We partnered with the local radio station, KFROG, which helped us bring in names such as Trace Adkins, Jennifer Nettles, The Band Perry, Thompson Square, Josh Turner, Scotty McCreery, Lauren Alaina, and Lee Brice. We hosted over 1,700 people at many of those concerts.

140

LEFT PAGE: *Jazz musician, Everette Harp, playing at Wilson Creek. RIGHT PAGE: TOP LEFT TO RIGHT: Country superstar, Trace Adkins. Lee Brice. Jennifer Nettles. MIDDLE LEFT TO RIGHT: Kodi Lee at a 2019 concert at the winery. Temecula Road performs live. BOTTOM: Big and Rich drew a crowd of over 1,750.*

Temecula Valley Symphony 2019

MORE CONSTRUCTION, MORE DEBT

In 2005 our tasting room became too crowded. We started setting up makeshift bars for the weekend crowds by putting wood planks on top of the wine barrels in the warehouse. We relocated the large wine tanks to the side patio to make room for more tasting bars. In the courtyard area, we built more patios and shaded areas for guests to gather.

Bill realized that our tasting room building wouldn't be able to handle the growing crowds. He envisioned a new, larger building that would also hold our offices and winemaking. He designed some preliminary plans with an architect and presented them to the family, but the estimated cost was $750,000. We wrestled with such a large project, but we knew we needed to expand. After much discussion, the family board approved it.

Over the next six months, the scope of the project grew. It now included a large ballroom, a catering kitchen, expanded barrel room, larger warehouse, bigger tank room, and an area for a new bottling line. The project estimate doubled to $1.5 million.

We learned that the county required even more parking and a more extensive septic system. I suggested we add more storage to the plans. Bill designed more office space. The project grew in scope and complexity—the updated cost: $3 million.

That's when Craig stepped in. He didn't want a repeat of the debacle he felt we had experienced when Bill acted as our general contractor, so he insisted we hire a professional general contractor with experience in large buildings.

The family agreed—the project was now too large for us to handle ourselves. We eventually hired a local developer who had recently built numerous high schools. But, hiring an outside company meant even higher costs. The board became alarmed at the escalating numbers as the expanded plans meant a much bigger debt load. The new price tag of $3 million caused some concern in the family as well. Could we handle the increased debt? We debated. Only one fact persuaded us to go forward: We were already bursting at the seams. We went ahead and broke ground on the new building in 2007.

Halfway through the building's construction, Mindy, our events manager, offered a suggestion: Why not add a restaurant to the project? She met with Bill and me in front of our almost-completed building and laid out her vision, "With all you're doing here as a winery, I think a restaurant would thrive."

"Yes," I responded, "but we would need a larger kitchen since we only built a small catering kitchen. And where do we put the restaurant? There's no room for a restaurant inside the new building."

"We would build it right here," Mindy said. We were standing on a dirt pad just in front of the partially-completed new building.

Bill caught Mindy's vision. "We could expand the kitchen by eliminating the area for the bottling line."

"I just don't see it yet," I said. "Where would the bottling line go?"

Mindy then took some wrought-iron patio chairs and marked the perimeter of what she envisioned as a patio for the restaurant.

CLOCKWISE FROM TOP LEFT: *Building progress in 2006. Family during construction. Balloons over the initial construction. The courtyard in 2020 on a cool Saturday in January. Tearing up the courtyard in 2006 after removing the large event tents we had up for six years.*

"Wow," I said, "that is way too big!" I imagined a smaller bistro concept. "It will take up most of the courtyard here. It'll stick out like a sore thumb."

"Trust me," Mindy said. "It's just the right size."

Bill moved some of Mindy's chairs. I assumed he was making the restaurant area smaller in agreement with me, but he moved the chairs *out* another ten feet to make it even bigger. "I like this size," he said. "Let's go for it." I just shook my head.

I went along with the idea but was concerned about how we would pay for it. Our architect would have to design it and, of course, we'd need more costly permits. Plus, one other small detail: we had never run a restaurant before.

The family decided to move forward. With the help of staff, we brainstormed names and ended up with the *Creekside Grille*. Bill also worked with the architect to tweak the plans to enlarge the ballroom, add more office space, expand the barrel room, and redesign the foyer with a spiral staircase.

Another unexpected expense slapped us in the face. We had done a lot of landscaping on the property, and the new building included a significant parking lot expansion. The county required us to post a bond equal to the value of the landscaping. The county valued all required landscaping at $125,000. We were forced to secure a bond for that amount before we could open the new phase. However, no bonding company would bond for that much, and we didn't have the funds.

A week later, Bill attended a function at City Hall and ran into Jim Carter, the owner of South Coast Winery, our neighbor, one mile to the west. Jim had heard about our predicament and, right there in the parking lot, offered to personally put up a $125,000 certificate of deposit. All we had to do was pay the interest, which would be relatively low. Bill was amazed that a competitor would offer to help. He was so overwhelmed at Jim's generosity that Bill shed a few tears—right there in the parking lot. We ended up not borrowing money from him as we were able to get another small construction loan, but we were so thankful for Jim's offer. That's the nature of the wine business—people helping people.

We completed the new building in 2008. By the time we increased the square footage, added the restaurant, expanded parking, put in more required hydrants and fire sprinklers, installed the winemaking equipment, furnished the building, and completed the courtyard landscaping, the price tag was somewhat different from the original $750,000. In short, over two years of tweaking the plans and expanding the project, the new total was approximately $7 million. We had no choice but to borrow more money.

Even though we incurred a significant new debt burden, we were hopeful the new building would pay for itself over time.

On September 15, 2008, we hosted our first event in the new *Champagne Ballroom*. It was a Monte Carlo Night fundraiser for the Temecula Valley Chamber of Commerce, and more than 250 guests attended. A marvelous beginning!

But as the event started, Bill received a phone call. He stepped out of the packed room to listen. He stood dumbfounded as he heard that the stock market had crashed for the third day in a row. The country was about to experience its worst economic crisis in nearly 80 years, and we were about to undergo a painful season that would test our family and business as never before.

148

2008 RECESSION

The day after we opened our new building, the local newspaper had two stories on the front page.

The top half read, "Dow Jones falls 750 points three consecutive days. China may come to the rescue. Will we have to speak Chinese soon?"

Below the fold was an article with the headline: "Wilson Creek Winery opens its new facility and restaurant."

The recession affected us in many ways. We knew that in tough economic times, people tend to give up luxury goods like wine. We were still receiving large numbers of guests, so we needed to maintain the same amount of staff. But those guests were tightening their wallets. Bill describes the change:

People used to say, "Boy, I really like that wine. I'll take two."

"Great. Two bottles, or two cases?"

"Two cases, of course. My business is growing, and my investments are doing well."

Then during the recession, the conversation changed:

"Boy I really like that wine, I'll take two."

"Great. Two bottles, or cases?"

"No, just two tastes. I just got laid off, and our house might be foreclosed."

About a third of our Wine Club members put their memberships on hold. Some called in tears, explaining that they didn't want to cancel, but they had to. Sales were declining. We did everything we could to cut expenses without hurting guest service. As a family, we were accustomed to tightening our belts; that's what we had done for the previous ten years.

MORE OUTSIDE HELP

This new building was the right move. We needed the room, but the project also resurrected some of the old family tensions. Craig and I feared that Bill's desire for growth, if unchecked, could bankrupt us. We felt Bill cut us out of the loop in much of the planning process, especially as the new building grew in scope. We all sensed that the way we were running the business as a family wasn't working anymore. It was time—again—to bring in another expert.

Over the next year, the recession also exposed areas where we lacked organization and efficiencies. So, in late 2009, the family brought in a consultant named John Ovrom. His specialty is going into companies and cleaning things up quickly.

John's first meeting with our family was a wake-up call. He said our company looked successful on the outside, but financially we were unhealthy. And if we didn't listen to his direction, the whole business could implode. We all saw the numbers and agreed we needed to take some drastic steps.

John had us sell off much of our wine inventory to reduce taxes and increase our depleted cash reserves. We sold cases valued at $500 for $40. We contacted local stores to take pallets of high-end red wines and sell them at a discount. The store managers were happy to do so; they could sell $50 bottles of wine for $20 and still make a profit.

John brought in a certified public accountant to help us get more organized. John also advised us to make a

clear distinction between the family and the business. For example, every winery truck, van, and piece of machinery was in my name—because I was the only one who had good credit when we bought the vehicles. The others had maxed out their credit cards to fund the business before I moved down in 1999. John helped us get these vehicles in the company name.

He advised us to cut unnecessary staff. He even told us to consider cutting some family members. If a family member was deemed unnecessary by John, the person needed to step up or step out. He helped us with succession planning, taxes, and clarifying individual roles. His cuts and changes were needed, but they were brutal.

It felt like John was pruning the winery, as a vineyard manager cuts back a vine. John pruned us as he reorganized the organizational chart. At the end of John's first year, Rosie, Deanna and Jenifer went to part-time. Libby felt it best to step out of her current, part-time role and focus on her family. I continued overseeing operations, and Bill continued as CEO.

Over the next two years, John realized that the family was, in fact, the number-one asset of the business. So, he kept us all involved in some capacity. Over time, we ended up liking John and his brutal honesty—so much so that we made him our part-time general manager for a while. We appointed him to our board, and he eventually became chairman, a seat he fills even to this day. John came to love our family, becoming one of our most passionate advocates, yet he is still brutally honest with us, which we need and appreciate.

LEFT PAGE: *Staff and family at an employee picking competition.* RIGHT PAGE: TOP LEFT TO RIGHT: *Sarah Wilson is our "Junior Lab Tech," with Gus and winemaking interns. Gerry with our vineyard team. Gus with Joe and Tim during crush. Joe is our Cellar Master who has worked in the wine industry for over 40 years.* MIDDLE: *Bill with John Ovrom. Mick chuckles while Bill coaches a newbie on what clusters to keep.* BOTTOM RIGHT: *The vineyard and winemaking teams after we received the award for the best wine in the valley for our 2013 Petite Sirah.*

*TOP TO BOTTOM: Libby and Rosie. Bill crowning Rosie on her birthday on October 14
which is right during crush, as you can tell by the looks of Bill's shirt.*

FIRING MOM

Rosie's love of cooking caused the daily lunches she prepared to expand from 12 to 40 people. She loves connecting with people, so preparing food for staff is fun for her. When problems arise, many of our staff go to Rosie and Gerry, viewing them as their surrogate mom and dad.

But when we built our new restaurant in 2008, the entire winery now had to adhere to the stricter restaurant health codes. Bill had to make a tough decision. Should he continue to let Rosie cook for the staff every day—or shut her down and run everything through the restaurant kitchen, as per the new health codes?

One day Bill approached Rosie while she was cooking in the tasting room kitchen. "Mom, you know we have chefs now. Why are you still feeding the staff?"

"I guess because they like it."

"Actually, you can't cook anymore. I'm sorry. All food is under the supervision of the executive chef in the new restaurant."

"I can still cook lunch in this kitchen right here in the tasting room, right?

Bill replied, "You can't cook anywhere on the winery property. There are new health codes."

"But this is my way to serve the staff and connect with everyone."

"I know, and I'm sorry. I appreciate what you've done, but I need you to stop cooking. You are done with cooking."

Rosie got in Bill's face. "So, are you firing me?"

"I guess I am. But now you can go back to your gardens and connect even more with the guests."

Rosie felt hurt. How could she contribute and still connect with guests? Rosie went back to trimming the flowers on the property and continued to make the cork necklaces we give to guests for special occasions. To this day, she personally delivers a bottle of sparkling wine with a handwritten note to every bride who gets married on our property. Rosie occasionally jumps behind the bar and pours tastes too. She loves to chat with people while she and Gerry eat lunch in the Creekside Grille every day. Looking back at her firing, Rosie comments, "I missed it for about a day, but I certainly don't miss all the food shopping and cleanup."

Her passion is her flowers. She describes one incident: "I was working in the gardens at the front entrance. An older woman came to me and asked, 'Do you work here?' I had on my Wilson Creek shirt and a straw hat trimmed with grapes and corks. I answered, 'Yes, I do.' A few minutes later, she again asked, 'Do you work here?' Again, I replied, 'Yes, I do.' A few minutes later the lady came back to Rosie and said, 'Do you work here? What do you do?' I blurted out, 'I own it!' Of course, I could have bitten my tongue. To this day I am a bit ashamed of being so rude and forward."

When we do family gatherings at Rosie and Gerry's house, Rosie loves to prepare homemade food. But she dislikes doing the dishes, so the deal has always been that she does all the cooking, and we kids clean it up. I visit Rosie and Gerry every Thursday night to connect over a bottle of wine. Almost every time, Rosie will whip up something for us to nibble on. You can take Rosie out of the kitchen, but you can't take the kitchen out of Rosie.

THE RED THREAD
AT THE REUNION

Two years ago, Libby chatted with classmates at her high school reunion held in the winery's Barrel Room. One particular friend made a comment that summarized our 20-year journey of running Wilson Creek. "Libby, I have known your family since the early days in South Pasadena. I attended most of your parties on Milan Avenue and even had dinner with your family a few times in your dining room. When I look around at what the Wilsons have accomplished in starting and building this winery, it reminds me of who you were as a family in South Pasadena. You hosted all kinds of people. You made anyone feel welcome. You were very active in the community. You were the central place in our city for people to gather and have fun. Your family is simply doing what you have always done but on a larger scale. Congratulations."

As I think back on our Midwest roots and our family experiences in Minnesota, South Pasadena, and Temecula, I see a red thread running through it all—a thread that will hopefully continue through the generations.

It is a thread that strives to embody authentic graciousness, warm hospitality, perseverance through difficulties, and compassion for others.

Hopefully, Wilson Creek Winery will continue to be a place and a community where others feel welcomed, loved, accepted, and valued. I am honored to write the story of our amazing family and how, together, we started a winery that surpassed our wildest dreams.

2019 Symphony

EPILOGUE

2000

2012

A Lasting Legacy

2010

Temecula Chamber Awards Gala

It is winter 2020, and four generations of Wilsons gather at Rosie and Gerry's house on the hill above the winery. Rosie prepares appetizers and a huge salad as Chris grills chicken on the patio barbecue. Dogs seem to be everywhere as Bill and Jenifer have brought their two goldens to play with Rosie and Gerry's two.

I look around and take it all in. It's been 20 years since we opened our doors. As a family, we continue to enjoy the winery and each other.

2002

2006

Winery

2019

I walk outside and see the tasting room expansion below. The number one criticism of our winery is still that we're too crowded. To remedy that, we recently expanded our tasting areas by adding more than 4,000 square feet. We converted what was initially slated to be Bill and Jenifer's home above the tasting room to a Wine Club lounge called the Upper Room. This area has two large bars, table seating for over 60, and balcony seating for 50 people. We also added a sit-down wine pairing area on the second floor, behind the Upper Room. We completed our Courtyard Bar and Grill where we serve gourmet pizzas, sandwiches, beer, and the popular sparkling wine slushies. I chuckle to myself that this whole venture started with a 20-foot tasting bar and two small restrooms.

Winemaking

In 2019, we were humbled to receive the award, *The Best Winery in the Inland Empire*, by the readers of *The Press-Enterprise*. This was the third time we received this prestigious honor. Our wines are winning awards, as many were rated 90+. We have become the valley's teaching winery as we host dynamic Wine Academy classes and professional wine certification courses. Greg (our vineyard manager since 2014) and Gus (our winemaker since 2013) teach wine courses at local colleges. The two also created a dynamic wine internship program with local, adult students.

Vineyards

I look out the other window at our meticulously maintained vineyards. Over the last seven years, our vineyard manager, Greg Pennyroyal, has improved the quality of our fruit by employing sustainable farming methods and restoring health to the vineyard ecosystem. These vines are now producing some of the best grapes in Southern California. Our vineyard team also manages another 100-plus acres off site. As our grapes get healthier, our wines are getting even better. Greg leads the Small Winegrowers Group, which has more than 100 members who gather monthly at the winery to learn how to manage their vines better. Additionally, Greg has introduced a cutting-edge agricultural technology into our vineyards called "regenerative agriculture" which goes beyond "sustainable."

LEFT PAGE: Greg teaching a class in pruning. Our vineyard crew. Pedro has been our foreman (middle with sunglasses) since 1999. RIGHT PAGE: Greg analyzing the topsoil.

166

Creekside Grille

I chuckle when I remember the idea of adding a small restaurant to the building blueprints when we built our large event and winemaking building in 2007. What I envisioned was a small bistro-style restaurant. Thanks to Bill, the plans got bigger and we designed a much larger venue. We opened the Creekside Grille in early 2009, and today it is one of the most popular restaurants in our valley. Guests rave about our Sunday brunch, and we are also proud of offering one of the best and safest gluten-free menus in the region.

LEFT PAGE: Rosie cooked lunch for the staff every day for nine years. RIGHT: Some of our kitchen staff with Executive Chef Steve Stawinski (center) in 2020.

168

Wilson Creek Manor

I look across the street and see the large home we acquired in 2015 when it was known as "The Castle." We remodeled the outside to make it look more like an Italian villa. When it first opened, the Wilson Creek Manor was a bed and breakfast consisting of nine rooms, each room with a private bathroom. Recently we converted it to a whole-house vacation rental where any group can rent it and have everything under one roof. There is also a pool, spa, game room, board room, grilling island, and a 1300-square-foot "Champagne Suite." The Manor is located right across the street from the winery.

LEFT PAGE: A bridal party enjoying The Manor. ABOVE: The Manor today.

Rosie and Gerry

Rosie and Gerry eat lunch every day at the winery and enjoy interacting with guests. They both turn 90 in 2020. They still travel to Europe with Deanna and me every year, as the four of us are wine hosts on annual wine river cruises. Rosie uses her golf cart to run their two golden retrievers. Gerry says, "Rosie and I get to live above the winery with our kids, grandkids, and great-grandkids within 15 minutes of the property. We wake up to hot air balloons in the morning, visit with wonderful people during the day, and enjoy sunsets at night. This is heaven on earth for us. We are truly living the dream."

LEFT PAGE: LEFT: Dancing at a Valentine's dinner at the winery. RIGHT: Rosie and Gerry on their second honeymoon in Tahiti. RIGHT PAGE: Rosie and Gerry with the dogs Sadie and Chablis.

Bill and Jenifer

I smile as I think about all the countless hours Bill and Jenifer have poured into this family venture. As our CEO, Bill is still the face and driver of the winery. He is part of the Temecula Convention and Visitors Bureau, the Rancho California Water District Board, and the Temecula Valley Winegrowers Association. Bill and Jenifer help with a local program to help foster kids called Rancho Damacitas. Their daughters, Cassidy and Cambria, are out of college and living nearby. Cassidy is working with a national wine sales company, and Cambria is an accomplished pastry chef. Some of her delicious creations are sold in our tasting room.

LEFT PAGE: Bill and Jenifer's wedding day. RIGHT PAGE: LEFT TO RIGHT: Cambria, Bill, Jenifer, Cassidy.

Mick and Deanna

Deanna and I are part of the leadership in a large local church. I also speak occasionally at other churches, where I bring "Vinny the Vine"—a 40-year-old Syrah vine that we had to uproot to make room for buildings. I decorate Vinnie with faux grape leaves and plastic grapes and use him to explain the powerful 15th chapter in the gospel of John, where Jesus teaches, "I am the vine, and you are the branches." Deanna continues to work for the winery as a part of our wine distribution team. Our daughter, Sarah, attends Great Oak High School in Temecula, where she plays varsity volleyball.

LEFT PAGE: LEFT: Mick speaking, with "Vinnie," at Journey Community Church in San Diego.
LEFT: 2003 wedding photo in the tasting room. RIGHT PAGE: A 2019 family photo.

Craig and Libby

My sister and her husband are still involved in the winery. They also volunteer for local Autism charities. Craig continues to serve on the winery board. Both their boys, Gavin and Hayden, are in college playing Division 1 baseball. Craig and Libby live ten minutes from the winery. Libby jokes that they have two goldens—a golden pug and a golden Chihauhau.

LEFT PAGE: Wedding photo in Foxborough with nieces and nephews (Heather on Craig's left).
RIGHT PAGE: 2019 family photo in the Upper Room. LEFT TO RIGHT: Gavin, Hayden, Libby and Craig.

1997

Heather and Luke

Heather lived on the property for over a decade but now has a home in town with her eight-year-old son, Luke. She loves family as she participates in all the inter-family functions and visits Rosie and Gerry often. Heather now lives only ten minutes away. She helps with Rosie and Gerry's healthcare, and she helps Rosie make all of the winery's cork necklaces.

LEFT PAGE: LEFT: Heather and Cambria. RIGHT: Heather with Deanna.
RIGHT PAGE: Heather and son Luke.

Chris and Jessica

Chris and Jess now have three children, Chloe (12), Crew (10), and Jett (3). Chris works full-time at the winery as a supervisor in our facilities department. They live just 15 minutes from the winery, and Jess works part-time as an interior designer and hairstylist. She has done makeup and hair for numerous brides at the winery.

LEFT PAGE: Chris working on the new tasting room construction. Mick officiating Chris and Jessica's wedding at the winery.

The Dogs and Pig

Rosie and Gerry have two goldens named Sadie and Chablis. Bill and Jenifer have two goldens named Tipsy and Sauvie. Our pig, Molly, has her own wine label called *Molly's Merlot*, but we recently gave her away to a local family who wanted her.

AN INTERVIEW *with Rosie and Gerry*

What do you think makes the winery such a great place to visit?

Gerry: Because Rosie and I are here (chuckle). Actually, it is our staff. They all understand the family feel. There is a feeling here that is different from some other places we have been. And that starts from the top down. And our staff have picked up on that. That is due to hiring good people and giving them our values. That family vibe permeates through the whole winery, and people sense it when they arrive. It is fun to walk around the property and hear the laughter.

People just love to talk about themselves—who doesn't? By connecting, we have a chance to ask them where they are from and all about themselves. That helps a lot, I think, being more interested in them than just selling them something. You can get good wine at a lot of places, but why do people come into our winery? It's for the experience, so you'd better give them a good experience.

Rosie: I think it's because all week long people get insincere service: *"Have a nice day!"* They don't look the guest in the eye, and it's just an impersonal corporate thing. Then they get here, and they meet the family, the owners, our dogs, and our friendly staff.

What qualified you to start a winery?

Gerry: Our only qualification was that we drank wine. We are not experts, so it was a lot of on-the-job training. We also hired people more experienced and smarter than we are.

What is it like running a wine business?

Gerry: As a young kid from Minnesota, who would have thought I would ever become involved in a winery? It's a real kick. The winery gives us a platform to be charitable and talk with people. I really feel we are helping people enjoy life. We get to talk with people from all over the world and hear their stories. It is like a party every day.

People are hungry for family in this society. People say, "Gosh, we wish we had some business of our own where we'd have all our kids because now our kids are scattered all over the world." We're in an ideal situation that a lot of people would love to have, and we're very conscious of that. Rosie and I have all of our children, grandchildren, and great-grandchildren living within 15 minutes of the winery. Our commute to work is 100 feet down the hill. We're very, very, very fortunate.

When we walk around, others give Rosie and me way too much credit for this place just because we're

the elders. I say, "My kids do all the work, and I come down and take the credit." To watch your own family take charge and do what they are doing makes us so darn proud. However, Rosie does an enormous amount of work around here too. An owner should be available and make himself or herself physically accessible, whether playing traffic cop, pointing out where the restrooms are, or whatever it is. It really is kind of goofy, but visitors act as if we're kind of special, and they want our picture and our autograph. I didn't do anything to deserve this, but that's beside the point. You're in the public eye, you have that position, and it still seems funny to me, but I'm happy to oblige.

What did your family do to build and maintain relationships?

Gerry: We always ate dinner as a family. I think relatives are important in this day and age. Even in a business situation, when we have a board meeting, we'll have dinner first, all together. I think family needs that association.

What was it like in the early struggling days of the winery?

Rosie: Not fun. If it were just Gerry and me, we probably would've walked away from the winery. But because there were eight adult family members, we all stuck together. That is why family is so important. It made the family more cohesive because we worked together. Not many families get that opportunity. Looking back, the struggle made us better. Had we started with a fortune and had no problems, we wouldn't have learned so much and still value what we have now.

What do you consider most important in life?

Gerry: I have come to realize that the quest for money should not be the driving force of your life. You can sit back and enjoy the same thing that anybody else in the world can—the sunrises, sunsets, just the beauty of the earth and being alive and enjoying your friends. We'll get a phone call from Mick, for example, who says, "Sunset alert!" and Rosie and I pause and pour a glass of wine and admire the sunset from our patio. Pretty soon "things" alone aren't that important. The Brink's truck doesn't follow the hearse. If you realize that things in and by themselves aren't that important, then you can enjoy what you do have. You can be more present in the moment.

How did you two get together?

Gerry: It ended up we were chasing each other, but initially, I wasn't looking. It quickly became apparent, and this has been verified over the years, that she was the one. I wanted someone whom I could look up to, that conversationally we didn't have to talk to each other to still enjoy just being together. Yet we could share each other's feelings, go through life together, and have so much fun doing that. When you share an experience with someone, it makes a world of difference. Fortunately, we liked the same things. I always said, at that age, how good is the judgment of a twenty-two-year-old boy? Guys can sometimes have the tendency to pick out women who look good but don't have that internal character and intelligence. With Rosie, I got both. And that was not a result of my skill and wisdom.

What is the secret to being married 67 years?

Gerry: One answer is to stay alive! A lot of good marriages didn't last because of health issues. You never know if that bullet is going to hit you. Rosie and I sit here and smile and say to each other, "Can you believe we are 90 years old?"

Rosie: Spoil each other. When a problem comes up, try to address it right away before it becomes a big problem. The key is to try to out-serve each other. Marriage is not fifty-fifty but eighty-eighty.

How did you handle hardship together?

Gerry: We lived through financial ups and downs, but that's just money. That could come and go. If there's any difficulty, you go through it together. Rosie's been an enormous help in being a good listener, and I listen to her. I've been very, very lucky there because Rosie's always expressed an interest in what I do. She's always looked for the good in situations and would tell me that things aren't as bad as I perceived. We are each other's best cheerleaders. We are a team. We are best friends. When I had low points, she was there for me and vice versa. We had our differences, but we worked through them.

What's it like getting older?

Gerry: Growing old is an adventure. It is something I've never done before (chuckle). I like to think of life as a long journey, but when you get toward the end and look back, you realize it's very short. People say that life is like a roll of toilet paper—the closer you get to the end, the faster it goes. Yet, even though it goes more rapidly, you appreciate every day that you are around. I want to slow down and enjoy every moment. As I get older, I face the reality that I won't live forever. So, I want to make the most of every moment and see each day as a gift.

Rosie: It is a blessing being around people all the time. We can't imagine ourselves sitting in rocking chairs looking at each other with nothing to do. Engaging with staff and guests stimulates our brains. With your mind, you use it or lose it.

Gerry on Rosie: This sounds like a cliché, but I've always had Rosie up on a pedestal. I so admire this woman that entered my life, and neither one of us ever dreamed we'd be sitting in a gosh darn winery! I truly married up. In short, I am a better person because of Rosie. I've always valued her spiritual outlook on life. I don't know anybody who has more depth of spiritual meaning than she has. I think there are more people who could probably quote the Bible better, but I do believe she lives it. What I dearly love about Rosie is she doesn't have an ounce of pretentiousness in her. What you see is what you get—not out to impress, and yet very impressive. She amazes me. She is my best friend.

Rosie on Gerry: Gerry came from four kids—I came from four kids. We were both middle-class. We were both raised Christian. We had so many similarities in our backgrounds that we didn't have a huge adjustment. Our biggest adjustment is—and I don't think Gerry will deny this—he's a "Neat Pete" and I'm a "Messy Bessie." He is my rock. Sometimes when I worry or get distracted, I can be like a balloon that floats away, and Gerry grabs the string, like, *"Not so fast!"*

Gerry has a wonderful personality. People gravitate to him. He's the best schmoozer in the world. He grounds me. Gerry gives me stability and free rein—up to a point, you know. If I want to do something crazy, then we discuss it. We discuss everything.

What is some final advice for your family and others?

Rosie: Talk things out as a family. Don't let money get in your way.

Gerry: Step out of your comfort zone and do new things rather than being a spectator in life. And yes, you can make a difference. Strive to give life, hope, grace, and love to others.

What do you want people to say at your memorial or celebration of life?

Rosie: I hope people would say, "She was a kick."

Gerry: I'd like to be remembered as a person who loved his wife, loved his family, and loved his country. Keep the funeral part short and the celebration long. Have a good party because it's a celebration.

Rosie: By the way, the older you get, the more you think about heaven.

Gerry: Without the reality of a real heaven and life after death, there is no real purpose in life. We are experiencing a taste of "heaven on earth" right now, but I'm looking forward to the real heaven as well.

Gerry and Rosie with grandkids in 2005. LEFT TO RIGHT: Cassidy, Hayden, Gavin, Rosie, Sarah, Gerry, Cambria.

Wilson Creek Winery's
Future Winery Owners

RIGHT: In 2018 we had a sewer system installed at the winery to replace our large septic system. The water district built a walled-in pump station in our lower parking lot. During construction the crew had to fill a large holding tank with clean water to check for leaks. When Bill saw this "sewer pool" he couldn't resist the photo opportunity. The pump station was designed to look like part of our winery architecture. So when guests ask Bill what the small building is in the lower parking lot, he responds with a smile, "That's where we keep the good s#@t."

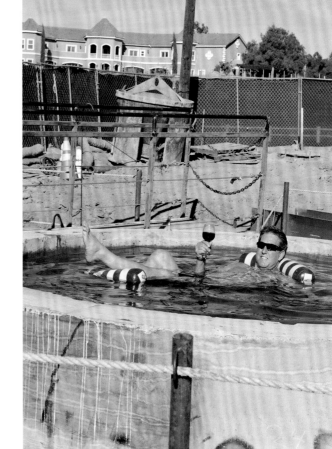

Since we grew up so close to Pasadena, we attended the Rose Parade every year. As teenagers, Bill, Libby and I camped out overnight every year to secure a spot on the route. We never imagined any family member would be in this prestigious parade until this last year when Rosie and Libby became part of the *Horsewomen of Temecula Wine Country* equestrian team. The team participated in numerous parades throughout 2019 to try to earn a spot in the 2020 Rose Parade. After they were officially invited, we raised money at a concert at the winery to help pay for the team to go. In the photo, Libby is sitting to the left of the driver. Rosie is in the front right of the carriage. Over 50 million viewers watch the parade annually. We received numerous calls and emails from friends who were thrilled to see Rosie and Libby.

190

When we designed the ten-foot *Legacy* monument to honor Rosie and Gerry, we wanted to inscribe on the back how we children, grandchildren and great grandchildren cherished Rosie and Gerry and desired to carry on their values and heart for others. The wording is below.

WILSON FAMILY LEGACY

Rosie and Gerry Wilson have had a dynamic impact
on numerous people and are leaving a profound impact on
their family and many others that will last from generation to generation.
They have imprinted on many hearts, immediate family
and extended family alike, a legacy of grace, compassion, faith,
humor, dependability, character, and love.
This wine was created to honor their lives, and this
monument was designed and built as a reminder of that
proud legacy and the great privilege and responsibility
we have as their children to carry on their amazing
legacy for generations to come.

AUTHOR

Mick is a co-owner of Wilson Creek Winery and Vineyards. He has a business degree from the University of Colorado, Boulder, and a Master of Divinity degree from Fuller Theological Seminary. Mick is a Certified Sommelier with the Court of Master Sommeliers, and a Certified Specialist of Wine with the Society of Wine Educators, and is credentialed with the Wine and Spirits Education Trust, Level II. Mick teaches numerous wine classes and speaks often at churches and leadership retreats. He lives in Temecula with his wife, Deanna, and daughter, Sarah.

ACKNOWLEDGMENTS

I thank my editor, Bill Ireland, who gave me the idea to make it a coffee-table book. He coached me in writing and deftly trimmed the manuscript from 70,000 words to 40,000.

Carrie Talbott VomSteeg, an area author/editor and leader of our local writer's group, was instrumental in the later stages of editing.

Two of the best local photographers, Justin Hulse and Randy Green, took numerous photos for this book.

Wendy Holder, the winery's VP of Marketing, skillfully did the book's layout.

I thank my brother Bill, who gave me the time to write this and pushed me along during the process.

I cherish the times spent with Rosie and Gerry hearing each story, some of which didn't make the final cut but will be in the extended version I will hand down to family. I often went back to them for clarification on specific details.

I am thankful for Rene Hader who taped interviews with every family member in 2006, compiling and transcribing over 30 hours of interviews.

Most of all, I thank my wife, Deanna, who continues to be my #1 cheerleader and encourager.

- Mick Wilson

WILSON CREEK

WINERY & VINEYARDS

35960 Rancho California Road
Temecula, California 92591
951.699.9463

WWW.WILSONCREEKWINERY.COM

PHOTO CREDITS

Cover: Justin Hulse (hulsephoto.com). Introduction:
Hulse. A MOMENT TO REFLECT: Family photo
by Randy Green (rkgreenstudios.com). Tasting room:
Hulse. Balloon: Rusty Manning. BEGINNINGS: Rosie
and Gerry in vines by Randy Green. ROSIE THE
HAM LADY: Ad from newspapers.com. MOVING
AND MOVING: Grapes photo by Hulse. TRAM-
POLINE: Grapes, Hulse. OLD 84 section: Photo of
Chris on tractor: Hulse. Grapes in DISCOVERING
BUBBLES: Hulse. Sarah with Mick: Melissa Jewel
Photography. FAMILY TENSION: Green. WE NEED
MORE LAND full page spread: Hulse. Three harvest
photos: Hulse. "Jazzing: Eric Darius photo by: Photos by
Ambrose. Temecula Symphony photos: Hulse. Bill with
mouse ears: *The Press-Enterprise / Southern California
News Group.* 2008 RECESSION: Hulse. THE RED
THREAD: Hulse. WINERY EPILOGUE: "Today"
photo from Hulse. MICK AND DEANNA: wedding
photo from Kathy Vasquez, family photo by Green. Dogs
in wine barrel: Randy Green. Rose Parade: Cowhand
Rockstar Photography.

REFERENCES

June 1996 article from *The Press-Enterprise /
Southern California News Group.* NEW PLAY-
ERS JOIN WINE COUNTRY article in *The
Californian*, March 9, 1998 by J.E. Mitchell.
WILSON FAMILY FOLLOWING THEIR
DREAM article by Karen Roberts in *Temecula
Today,* July 2002 issue. Photo of Rosie and Gerry
on the cover of the *Temecula Today* magazine by
Temecula Chamber of Commerce.

Temecula Valley info references: Wikipedia,
VisitTemeculaValley.com, Temecula Wine
Country—History and Facts by Kay Syrah, blog
posted August 10, 2018.

"Most Popular Winery" denotes that Wilson
Creek was awarded the Readers' Choice Award
from the *The Press-Enterprise* in 2016, 2017,
2018, 2019, and voted the Best Winery in the
Inland Empire in 2015 and 2019.